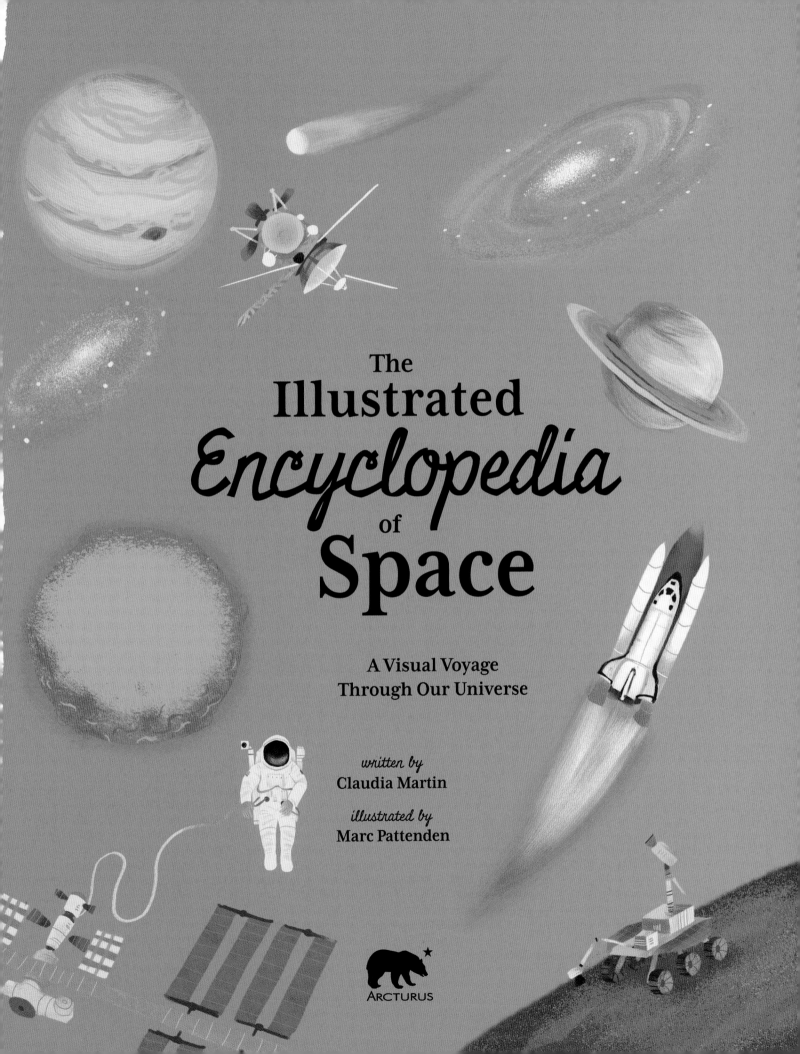

The
Illustrated
Encyclopedia
of
Space

A Visual Voyage
Through Our Universe

written by
Claudia Martin

illustrated by
Marc Pattenden

ARCTURUS

A note on large numbers:

1 million	1,000,000
1 billion	1,000,000,000
1 trillion	1,000,000,000,000
1 quadrillion	1,000,000,000,000,000
1 quintillion	1,000,000,000,000,000,000
1 sextillion	1,000,000,000,000,000,000,000
1 septillion	1,000,000,000,000,000,000,000,000

ARCTURUS

This edition published in 2024 by Arcturus Publishing Limited
26/27 Bickels Yard, 151–153 Bermondsey Street,
London SE1 3HA

Author: Claudia Martin
Illustrator: Marc Pattenden
Designer: Rocket Design (East Anglia) Ltd
Consultant: Dr. Helen Giles
Star maps on pages 62–63 courtesy of Shutterstock/oxameel

ISBN: 978-1-3988-3678-5
CH010465US
Supplier 29, Date 0124, PI 00005054

Printed in China

Contents

Super Space

Spinning in space is a small, rocky planet that we call Earth. This beautiful planet is just one of trillions of planets in the vast Universe. The Universe is everything that we know to exist, from planets to shining stars, from moons to great galaxies.

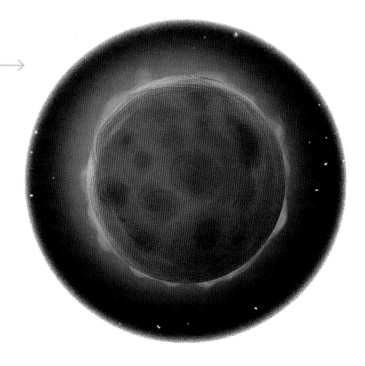

STARS

A star is a ball of glowing gas. Most stars are so massive that they have immense gravity. Gravity is a force that pulls all objects toward one another, but the more massive the object, the stronger the pull of its gravity. A star's gravity can hold objects such as planets around it, and keep them moving in roughly circular paths called orbits.

PLANETS

Planets are large objects that usually orbit a star. The strength of a planet's own gravity has pulled it into a ball-like shape. While some planets are made of rock and metal, others are made of swirling gas and liquid.

DWARF PLANETS

Dwarf planets are smaller than true planets. Like true planets, dwarf planets orbit a star. Their gravity is strong enough to pull them into a rounded shape, although many are not perfect balls. Unlike true planets, dwarfs are too small for their gravity to clear other large objects out of their orbit.

MOONS

Moons are objects that orbit a planet, a dwarf planet, or even a smaller object such as an asteroid. Moons are held in orbit by the larger object's gravity. When a moon is less than 1 km (0.6 miles) across, it is sometimes called a moonlet.

GALAXIES

A galaxy is a collection of stars, planets, gas, and dust, held together by gravity. Galaxies are usually in groups, known as galaxy clusters, which form part of even larger groups, known as superclusters.

VAST DISTANCES

In this book, we measure distances in our Solar System in kilometers (km) and miles. Beyond the Solar System, distances are so huge that measurements are given in light-years. One light-year is how far light travels in one year—9.46 trillion km (5.88 trillion miles). If a star is 1 million light-years away, its light has taken 1 million years to reach us. In fact, our eyes are seeing the star as it was 1 million years ago—so perhaps the star does not even exist any more.

The Big Bang

Around 13.8 billion years ago, the Universe began with an event that astronomers call the Big Bang. We do not know if anything existed before the Big Bang, but we do know that, in the first moment of the Big Bang, the Universe started to expand from a tiny point—and it has been getting bigger ever since.

At first, the Universe was an incredibly hot, tightly packed point that astronomers now call the "singularity." As the Universe expanded from the singularity, it cooled. After 1 second, the Universe was 200 trillion km (124 trillion miles) wide and 10 billion °C (18 billion °F). Today, the Universe that we can see (known as the observable Universe) is 900 sextillion km (560 sextillion miles) wide. Its average temperature is -270 °C (-454 °F).

In its first moments, the Universe contained no matter. Matter is anything, from people to stardust, that has mass (weight). But less than a second after the Big Bang, the first matter came into being—tiny particles. After thousands of years, these particles came together to form the first atoms, which are the building blocks for all ordinary matter in the Universe. Over the next millions and billions of years, stars, galaxies, and planets formed.

380,000 YEARS

Protons, neutrons, and electrons come together to make the first atoms. Atoms have a nucleus (middle) containing protons and neutrons, circled by electrons. The earliest atoms are the lightest and simplest atoms—hydrogen and helium. Now the Universe has clouds of hydrogen and helium atoms, which form floating gases.

0.0001 SECONDS

As the Universe cools, the conditions become right for the first matter to form. Tiny particles appear, far too small to be seen by the human eye. The particles include protons, neutrons, and electrons.

0 SECONDS

Space and time come into being with an explosion too powerful to imagine. In the first fractions of a second, the Universe doubles in size again and again, then its growth slows.

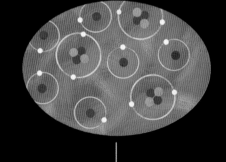

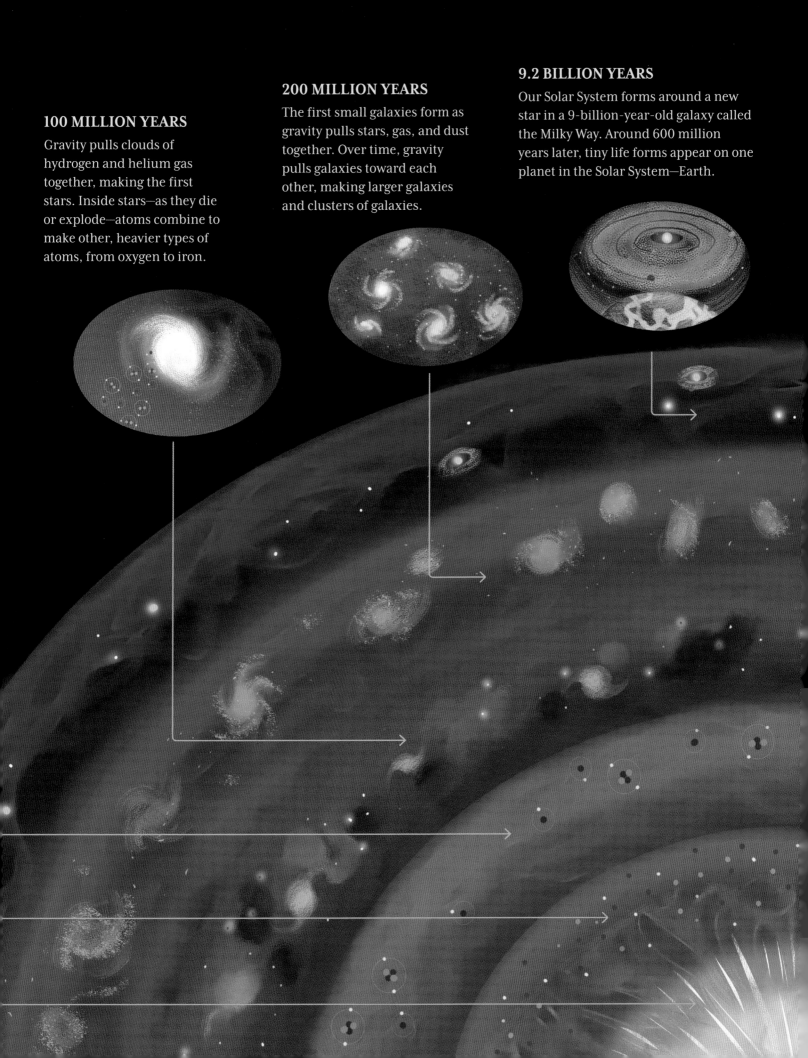

100 MILLION YEARS

Gravity pulls clouds of hydrogen and helium gas together, making the first stars. Inside stars—as they die or explode—atoms combine to make other, heavier types of atoms, from oxygen to iron.

200 MILLION YEARS

The first small galaxies form as gravity pulls stars, gas, and dust together. Over time, gravity pulls galaxies toward each other, making larger galaxies and clusters of galaxies.

9.2 BILLION YEARS

Our Solar System forms around a new star in a 9-billion-year-old galaxy called the Milky Way. Around 600 million years later, tiny life forms appear on one planet in the Solar System—Earth.

The Solar System

At the heart of the Solar System is the Sun. It is a star, a sphere of hot gas. At 1,390,000 km (864,000 miles) wide, the Sun is the largest object in our region of space, until the next star, which lies more than 40 trillion km (25 trillion miles) away. Massive objects have powerful gravity, which is the force that pulls all objects toward each other. The pull of the Sun's gravity holds trillions of other objects around it, and most of them are moving around the star in roughly circular paths called orbits. Together, the Sun and these objects are known as the Solar System.

The seven largest objects orbiting the Sun are the seven largest planets. The biggest of all of these is the giant planet Jupiter. The eighth and smallest planet, Mercury, is smaller than the Solar System's two largest moons, Ganymede and Titan. Moons are objects that orbit a planet, held by the strength of their planet's gravity. Orbiting the Sun itself are also at least nine—and perhaps many more—dwarf planets, which are smaller than true planets, but still have enough gravity to pull them into a rounded shape.

Around 4.6 billion years ago, the Solar System formed from a cloud of dust and gas. Perhaps shaken by the explosion of a nearby star, the cloud collapsed into a flat, spinning disk. Gravity pulled more and more material into the core of the disk. Here, the pressure grew so intense that hydrogen atoms started to smash together, forming a different type of atom—helium—and releasing energy that we can see as light and feel as heat. This was the birth of the Sun, which has shone ever since. Clumps formed in the remaining disk, eight of them growing large enough to become planets. Smaller clumps became moons, dwarf planets, rocky asteroids, and fiery comets.

Sun   Mercury   Ganymede   Pluto

The Sun is 285 times wider than Mercury, the smallest planet. At 4,880 km (3,032 miles) across, Mercury is 2,504 km (1,556 miles) wider than the largest dwarf planet, Pluto, but 388 km (241 miles) less wide than the largest moon, Jupiter's Ganymede.

The Solar System took shape from a spinning disk of gas and dust, with the bright Sun at its core. The disk spun counterclockwise (anticlockwise), which is why all the planets still orbit the Sun in that direction.

The Sun's Family

From nearest to farthest from the Sun, the planets are Mercury, Venus, Earth, Mars, Jupiter, Saturn, Uranus, and Neptune. On Mercury, the Sun appears three times larger than when it is viewed from Earth. From Neptune, the Sun would look one-thirtieth the size it appears from Earth.

The four inner planets—Mercury, Venus, Earth, and Mars—are made of metal and rock. As the Solar System formed, only these materials—which do not melt until they get extremely hot—could stay solid so close to the Sun. The inner planets are smaller than the outer planets, because there was less of these materials to go around. Due to their small size, the inner planets have weaker gravity than the outer planets, so they are not orbited by ring systems or many, if any, moons.

The outer planets are made of materials such as hydrogen and methane, which turn easily to gas. As the Solar System formed, the Sun blew these gassy materials into the Outer Solar System, where they formed the four giant planets. None of the outer planets has a solid surface—they are mostly gas and liquid.

MERCURY

Not much bigger than Earth's Moon, Mercury is the smallest planet. It also has the fastest orbit, moving at an average speed of 170,486 km/h (105,935 miles per hour).

VENUS

Venus is the second largest of the inner planets, with almost as great a size and mass (or weight) as Earth. Along with Mercury, it is one of the two planets with no moons.

EARTH

The largest inner planet, Earth, is nearly three times wider than Mercury. Earth is the only Solar System planet that is known to be home to living things.

SATURN

The second largest planet has a larger ring system than any other planet. Although Saturn is not suitable for life, some of its 146 moons might be.

MARS

Mars is the inner planet with the most moons—two. At Mars's closest approach to Earth, it is 57.6 million km (35.8 million miles) away, around 20 million km (12 million miles) farther away than Venus when it passes us.

NEPTUNE

Neptune has the slowest orbit of the eight planets, moving at an average speed of 19,548 km/h (12,147 miles per hour). The only Solar System planet that can never be seen without a telescope, it was the last to be discovered, in 1846.

JUPITER

The largest planet, Jupiter, is thirty times wider than the smallest planet, Mercury. Jupiter's mass is 2.5 times the mass of all the other planets combined.

URANUS

The third largest planet is slightly wider than Neptune, but has a lower mass. Although Uranus is faintly visible to the human eye, it was the first planet to be discovered using a telescope, in 1781.

The Sun

**The Sun is a medium-sized star, one of more than 100 billion stars in the Milky Way Galaxy.
Our star has been shining for around 4.6 billion years—and will shine for another 5 billion years.
It supplies Earth with the perfect amount of light and heat to make our planet suitable for life.**

BALL OF PLASMA

More than two-thirds of the Sun's mass is hydrogen gas, while the rest is mostly helium gas. Yet this is not ordinary gas, like the air we breathe on Earth. It has turned to plasma. Like everything from people to planets, plasma is made of atoms. In plasma, the atoms are so hot they have broken apart, releasing particles called electrons. Since electrons carry a tiny electric charge, plasma also has an electric charge.

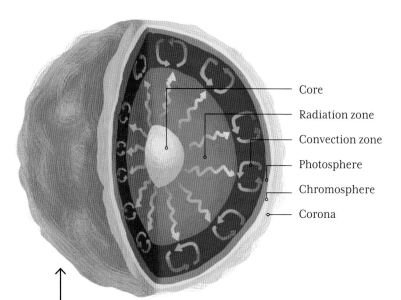

Core
Radiation zone
Convection zone
Photosphere
Chromosphere
Corona

Although the photosphere is no more solid than the rest of the Sun, beneath this layer the star is opaque (not see-through). This makes the photosphere the star's visible surface.

ENERGY JOURNEY

Every second, the Sun gives off enough energy to power all the machines on Earth for 500,000 years. This energy begins its journey in the Sun's core. Here, hydrogen atoms fuse into helium atoms. This process is called nuclear fusion. It will continue for another 5 billion years, when the Sun will run out of hydrogen and start to die (see page 70), destroying all the planets.

Nuclear fusion releases energy in the form of tiny particles called photons. The photons travel outward through the Sun's layers, passing first through the radiation zone. Here the photons move by a process called radiation—they bounce from atom to atom. Next, the photons travel through the convection zone, moving through a process called convection—they are carried by currents of hot plasma, which rise, cool, then sink.

After thousands of years, the photons reach the Sun's surface, the photosphere. Now they travel through the layers of gas that form the Sun's atmosphere—the chromosphere and corona—and out into space.

WONDERFUL WAVES

When the Sun's photons reach Earth, about 8 minutes after leaving the star, we see some as light and feel some as heat. Yet light and heat are only a part of the energy given off by the Sun. Photons carrying less energy form radio waves and microwaves, while high-energy photons form ultraviolet, X-rays, and gamma rays. All the forms of the Sun's energy are together known as the electromagnetic spectrum.

The Sun Facts

OBJECT	Star
MASS	333,000 Earths
SIZE	1.39 million km (0.86 million miles) across
ROTATION	Around 27 days
TEMPERATURE	15 million °C (27 million °F) at the core; 5,500 °C (9,930 °F) at the photosphere
LOCATION	28,000 light-years from the middle of the Milky Way Galaxy

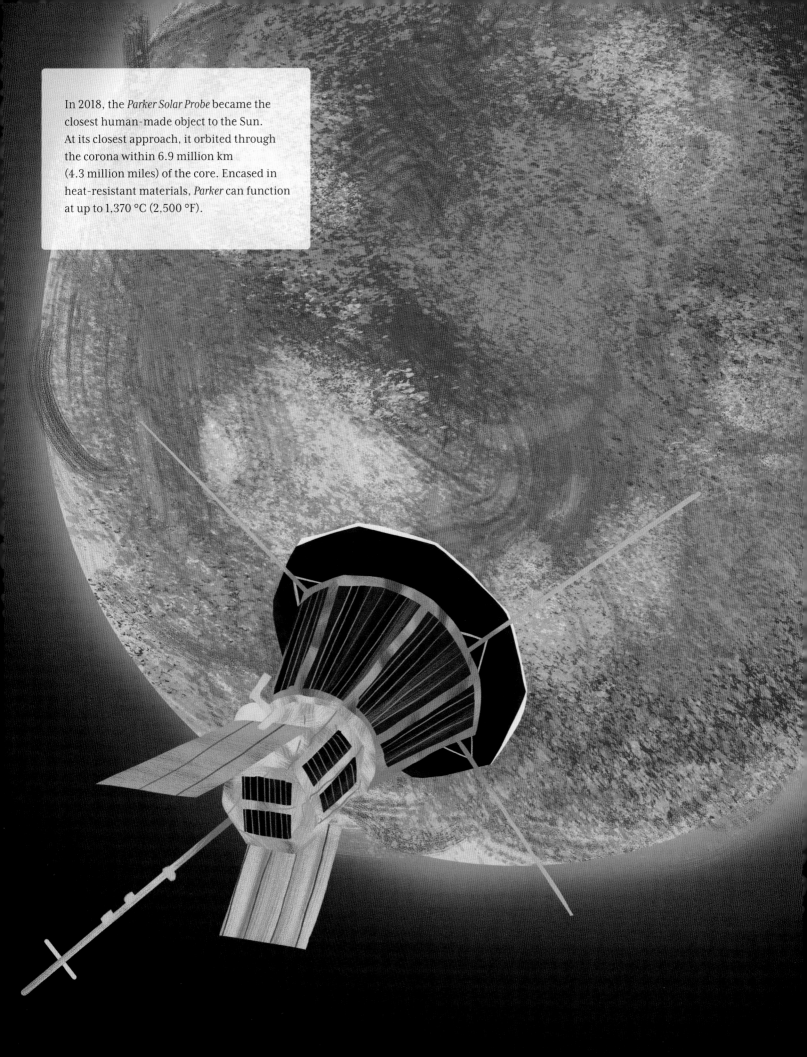

In 2018, the *Parker Solar Probe* became the closest human-made object to the Sun. At its closest approach, it orbited through the corona within 6.9 million km (4.3 million miles) of the core. Encased in heat-resistant materials, *Parker* can function at up to 1,370 °C (2,500 °F).

The Sun's Activity

The Sun's appearance changes constantly. Coming and going are dark spots, known as sunspots, as well as flares and loops. This activity can be viewed only using special equipment—never look directly at the Sun, as its brightness can cause blindness.

MAGNETIC FIELDS

The Sun's activity is caused by its magnetic fields, which are areas with powerful magnetic force. On Earth, we know magnetism as a force that makes magnets attract (pull) or repel (push away) each other. Magnetism can be caused by the movement of electric charges. Since the Sun's plasma is electrically charged (see page 12), its movements create moving magnetic fields.

As the Sun's magnetic fields tangle, cross, and stretch, plasma and energy erupt from the Sun's surface. Over an 11-year period, known as the solar cycle, this activity peaks, then calms. At the peak, there may be around 150 sunspots on the photosphere. At the Sun's calmest, there may be just one or two. When solar activity peaks, more intense auroras (see page 28) can also be seen in Earth's skies.

SUNSPOTS

Sunspots appear darker than the surrounding photosphere because they are cooler. They last for a few days or weeks, appearing where magnetic fields are particularly strong, which prevents some of the Sun's heat reaching the surface.

A sunspot has a dark central area, known as the umbra, which is surrounded by a less dark, warmer area known as the penumbra. The temperature of an umbra can be around 3,500 °C (6,330 °F)—about 2,000 °C (3,600 °F) less hot than the rest of the photosphere.

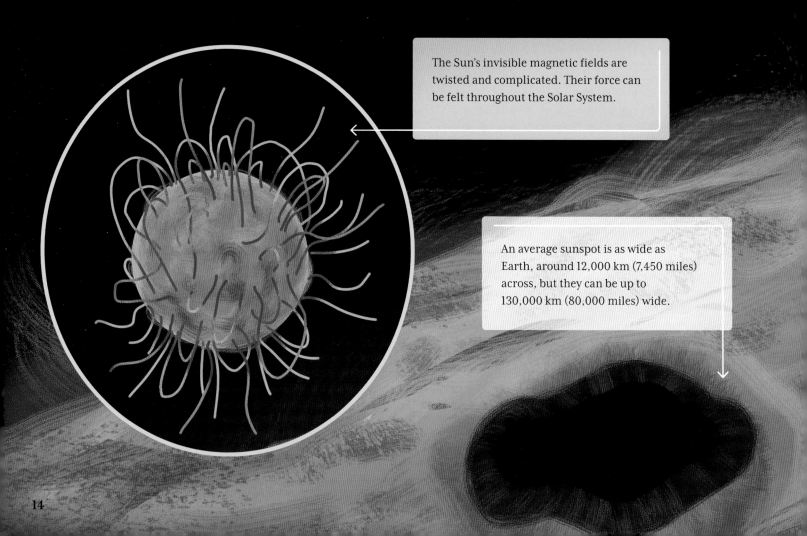

The Sun's invisible magnetic fields are twisted and complicated. Their force can be felt throughout the Solar System.

An average sunspot is as wide as Earth, around 12,000 km (7,450 miles) across, but they can be up to 130,000 km (80,000 miles) wide.

LOOPS AND FLARES

Loops happen when a loop of magnetic field drags a curl of plasma into the corona. Loops often erupt from areas of the photosphere with lots of sunspots. Flares happen when magnetic fields suddenly either cross or untangle, creating an explosion of plasma and energy.

Major flares often happen at the same time as coronal mass ejections (CMEs), which are bubbles of intense energy that explode into space at up to 11 million km/h (7 million miles per hour). When solar activity is at its peak, there may be three CMEs per day. On Earth, unusually intense CMEs can cause problems with radio communication. In 1859, a massive CME damaged electrical systems, making some spark into flame.

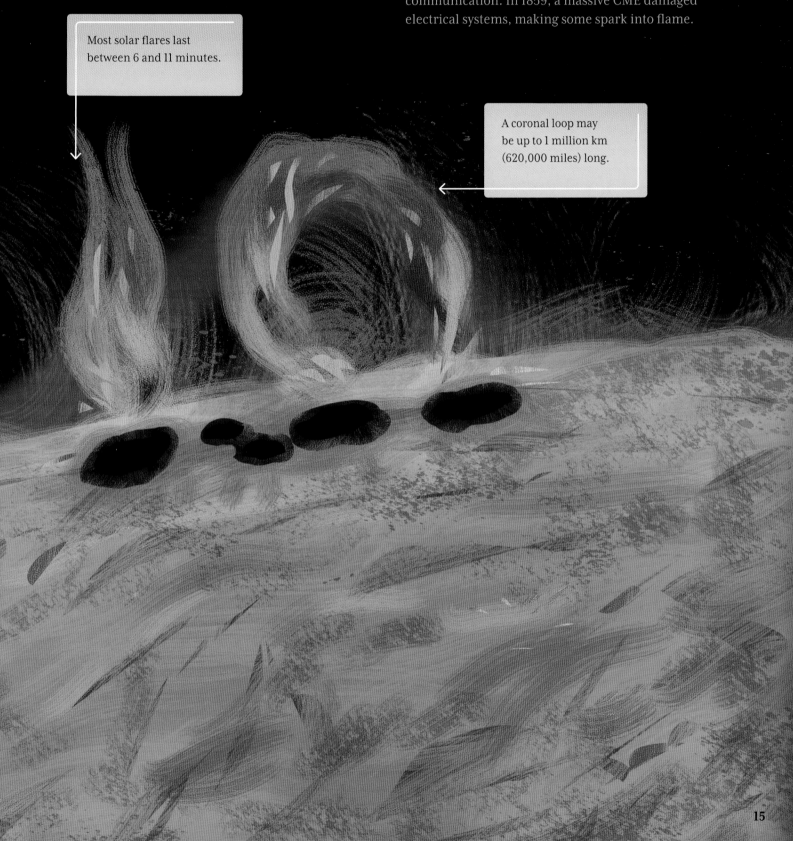

Most solar flares last between 6 and 11 minutes.

A coronal loop may be up to 1 million km (620,000 miles) long.

Mercury

Mercury is named after the Roman messenger god, known for his swift journeys. The planet's journey around the Sun is so fast that it makes one orbit in about 88 Earth days. This planet has been watched by humans since ancient times, even though its closeness to the Sun makes it difficult to see.

LOOKING FOR MERCURY

Like the other planets, Mercury does not give off light, but can be seen from Earth because sunlight reflects off its surface. It looks like a yellowish "star." During parts of the year, the planet can be seen in the west, just after sunset. At other times, it can be seen just before sunrise, near where the Sun will rise in the east.

FAST AND SLOW

The closer an object is to the Sun, the more it feels the pull of the Sun's gravity. As the closest planet to the Sun, Mercury orbits faster than the other planets so that it is not pulled into the star. This is like a cyclist peddling round the steeply sloping, curving track of a cycling arena. If the cyclist keeps peddling fast, they will not fall down the slope—but as soon as they slow down, gravity pulls them downhill.

Like all the planets, Mercury also rotates, turning around its own axis (an invisible line running through its poles). The Sun's intense gravity slows Mercury's rotation, so it spins just once every 59 Earth days. In fact, three Mercury days (rotations) are exactly equal to two Mercury years (orbits).

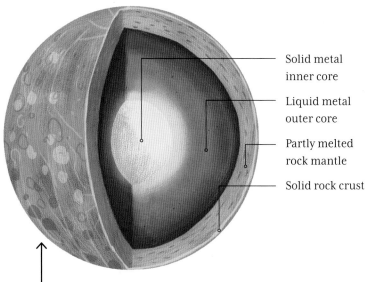

Solid metal inner core

Liquid metal outer core

Partly melted rock mantle

Solid rock crust

Mercury's metal core is around 2,000 °C (3,600 °F). It is surrounded by partly melted rock, known as the mantle, which is topped by a solid rock crust.

LITTLE ATMOSPHERE

Earth has a thick atmosphere, a blanket of gases held by the planet's gravity. Mercury has almost no atmosphere as its gravity is too weak to hold on to much gas so near the Sun. The Sun heats Mercury's surface to 427 °C (800 °F) during the day. Yet without an atmosphere to hold in heat, at night Mercury's surface falls to -179 °C (-290 °F). These extreme temperatures make Mercury unsuitable for life.

Mercury's lack of an atmosphere also meant that there was nothing to slow down space rocks as they battered the planet during the early years of the Solar System. As a result, the planet has more impact craters—bowl-shaped dips caused by crashes with asteroids and comets—than any other planet. Mercury has thousands of craters, the largest of them, called the Caloris Basin, is 1,550 km (960 miles) across.

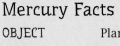

Mercury Facts

OBJECT	Planet
MASS	0.055 Earths
SIZE	4,880 km (3,032 miles) across
MOONS	0
ROTATION	59 days
ORBIT	88 days
TEMPERATURE	An average of 167 °C (333 °F) on the surface
LOCATION	An average of 57.9 million km (36 million miles) from the Sun

Mercury has been visited by fewer space probes than the other inner planets, because it orbits the Sun so quickly that a probe needs to travel very fast to meet it, then brake sharply to resist the Sun's pull. The *MESSENGER* probe was the first to orbit Mercury, in 2011–2015.

Venus

Although it is the second closest planet to the Sun, Venus is the hottest planet in the Solar System due to its thick atmosphere. Venus is also the only planet that rotates more slowly than it orbits the Sun, meaning that a Venus day is longer than a Venus year.

BEAUTIFUL AND DEADLY

Venus is named after the Roman goddess of beauty. Since the planet is the brightest object in Earth's night sky after the Moon—and can even sometimes be seen in daylight—the planet has been watched or worshipped by many peoples since ancient times. Venus's brightness is due to sunlight reflecting off its thick clouds.

For much of the year, Venus can be seen in either the evening or early morning sky, never appearing to move far from the Sun since it orbits closer to the star than we do.

While clouds on Earth are made of water drops, Venus's clouds are made of drops of sulfuric acid. On Earth, this dangerous acid is used to clean drains. These clouds float in Venus's thick atmosphere, which is mostly carbon dioxide. This gas traps the Sun's heat, making it hot enough on Venus's surface to melt metals such as lead.

Venus's terrific heat (which would boil away any water) and its carbon dioxide atmosphere (which would be deadly to animals in such quantities) make it completely

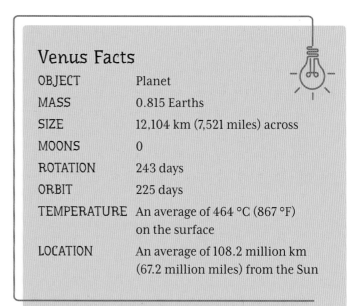

Venus Facts

OBJECT	Planet
MASS	0.815 Earths
SIZE	12,104 km (7,521 miles) across
MOONS	0
ROTATION	243 days
ORBIT	225 days
TEMPERATURE	An average of 464 °C (867 °F) on the surface
LOCATION	An average of 108.2 million km (67.2 million miles) from the Sun

unsuitable for life. The longest any space probe has functioned on Venus's hostile surface is 127 minutes, a time achieved by the *Venera 13* probe in 1982.

WRONG DIRECTION

All the Solar System planets orbit counterclockwise (anticlockwise) and all except Venus and Uranus also rotate counterclockwise when viewed from above their north pole. Venus rotates clockwise, but it must originally have rotated the other way, since it formed in a counterclockwise-spinning disk. If the disk had spun the other way, the planets would orbit and rotate the other way, too. In addition to rotating the wrong way, Venus also rotates more slowly than any other Solar System planet, each spin taking 243 days.

Astronomers believe that, early in its life, Venus must have been hit by a planet-sized object, which reversed its rotation or even flipped it upside down. Since Venus rotates the opposite way from Earth, on Venus the Sun appears to rise in the west and set in the east. However, the planet's clouds would always block any view of the Sun from the surface.

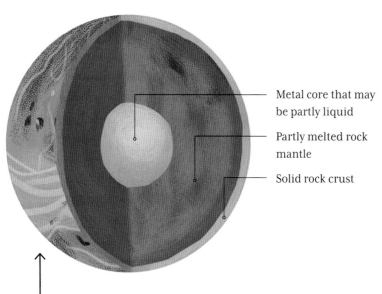

Metal core that may be partly liquid

Partly melted rock mantle

Solid rock crust

Venus has a rocky crust marked by mountains, plains, and impact craters. Beneath the crust is a mantle of denser rock, 2,840 km (1,760 miles) thick, surrounding a metal core of iron and nickel.

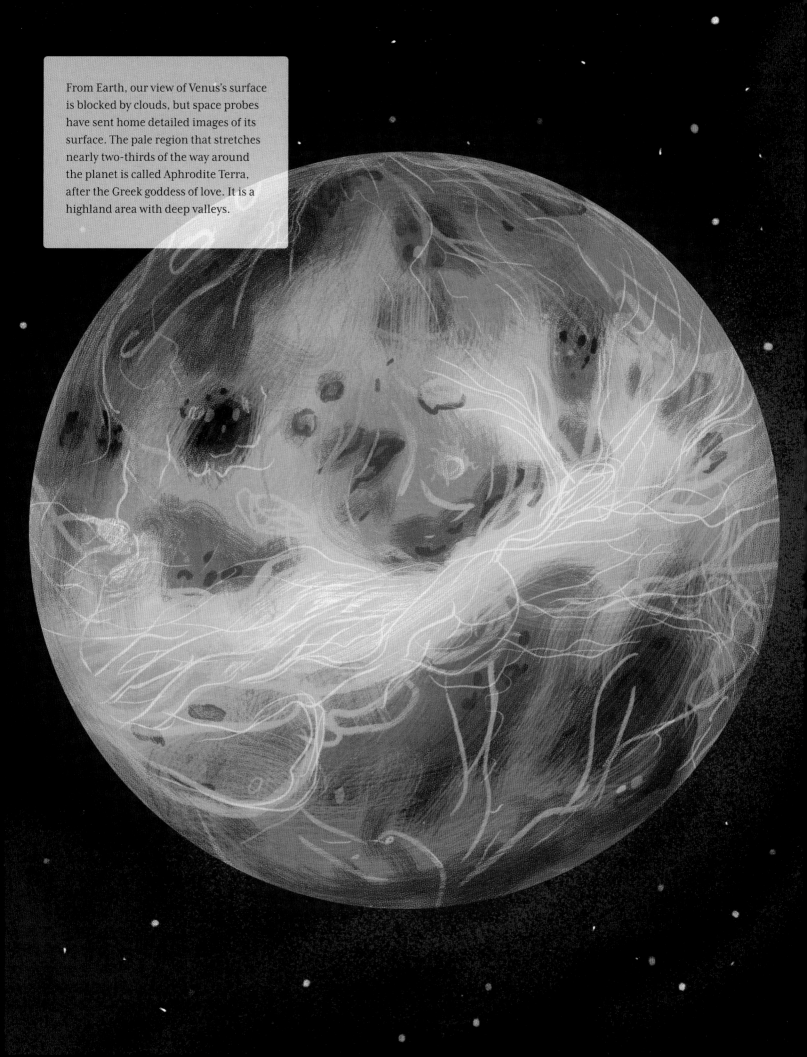

From Earth, our view of Venus's surface is blocked by clouds, but space probes have sent home detailed images of its surface. The pale region that stretches nearly two-thirds of the way around the planet is called Aphrodite Terra, after the Greek goddess of love. It is a highland area with deep valleys.

Venus's Volcanoes

With more than 1,600 major volcanoes and many smaller ones, Venus has more volcanoes than any other planet in the Solar System. Around 167 of its volcanoes are over 100 km (62 miles) wide. Most of Venus's volcanoes are no longer erupting, but astronomers think some may still be active.

MAKING VOLCANOES

Volcanoes are holes in a planet or moon's crust where melted rock from the mantle, known as magma, flows to the surface. Once magma has erupted from a volcano, it is known as lava. It cools into solid rock. Due to its many volcanoes, two-thirds of Venus's surface is covered by dried lava.

Venus's volcanoes formed in a different way from most of Earth's volcanoes. On Earth, most volcanoes form at the edges of tectonic plates, which are the giant, jagged-edged plates of rock that make up Earth's crust. These volcanoes were made as tectonic plates pushed together or moved apart, forcing magma to the surface. However, Venus's crust is not broken into tectonic plates. Its volcanoes formed where red-hot magma simply rose up through cracks in the crust. A few volcanoes on Earth are formed by the same process, including Mauna Loa—on the Island of Hawaii, in the Pacific Ocean—which is Earth's widest active volcano at 120 km (75 miles) across.

WIDE MOUNTAINS

Like most volcanoes on Earth, some of Venus's volcanoes have taken the shape of mountains, as layer after layer of lava cooled, hardened, and built up. The highest volcano on Venus, Maat Mons, formed in this way. It rises 5 km (3 miles) above the surrounding plain, and is 395 km (245 miles) wide. The very widest of the planet's mountain volcanoes, Theia Mons, is around 800 km (500 miles) wide.

Crown-like volcanoes range from 60 to 1,000 km (35 to 620 miles) wide.

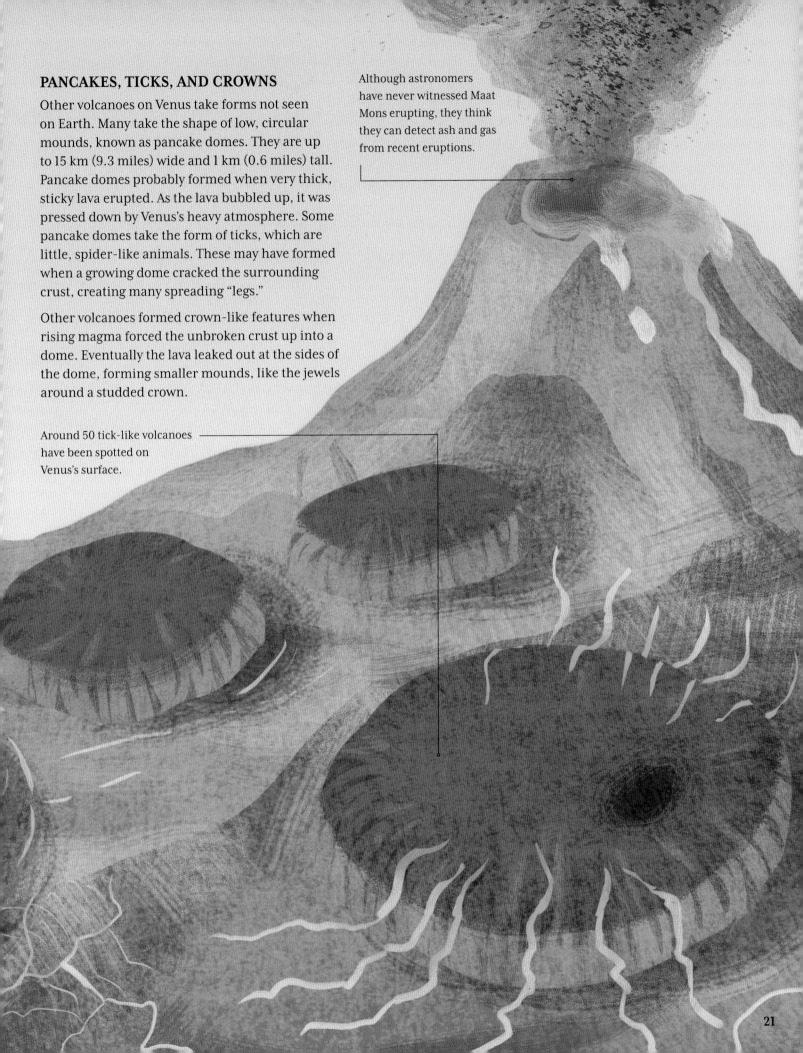

PANCAKES, TICKS, AND CROWNS

Other volcanoes on Venus take forms not seen on Earth. Many take the shape of low, circular mounds, known as pancake domes. They are up to 15 km (9.3 miles) wide and 1 km (0.6 miles) tall. Pancake domes probably formed when very thick, sticky lava erupted. As the lava bubbled up, it was pressed down by Venus's heavy atmosphere. Some pancake domes take the form of ticks, which are little, spider-like animals. These may have formed when a growing dome cracked the surrounding crust, creating many spreading "legs."

Other volcanoes formed crown-like features when rising magma forced the unbroken crust up into a dome. Eventually the lava leaked out at the sides of the dome, forming smaller mounds, like the jewels around a studded crown.

Although astronomers have never witnessed Maat Mons erupting, they think they can detect ash and gas from recent eruptions.

Around 50 tick-like volcanoes have been spotted on Venus's surface.

Earth

No more than 100 million years after the Sun's birth, our planet took shape from dust and gas. Then, around 200 million years later, Earth was joined by its companion, the Moon. Slowly, our red-hot planet cooled until it was a suitable home for life.

A GROWING CLUMP

As the disk of gas and dust (see page 8) spun around the young Sun, particles bumped and stuck together. The gravity of these particles pulled in other particles, and all the crashing made the clump super-hot, up to 10,000 °C (18,000 °F). By around 4.5 billion years ago, the clump was a planet-sized sphere of molten, mixed-together rock and metal.

A CRASH

The early Solar System was more disordered than today. A smaller planet—which astronomers call Theia—was probably tugged or thrown into Earth. The crash shattered Theia and flung rubble into space. Pulled by Earth's gravity, the rubble formed an orbiting sphere of rock and metal— the Moon.

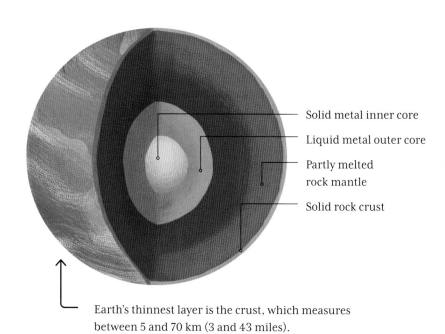

Solid metal inner core
Liquid metal outer core
Partly melted rock mantle
Solid rock crust

Earth's thinnest layer is the crust, which measures between 5 and 70 km (3 and 43 miles).

COOLING DOWN

Since metal is heavier than rock, Earth's molten metal sank, while its liquid rock rose toward the surface. The metal formed our planet's core of iron and nickel. The core was wrapped by a thick layer of dense rock, known as the mantle. Lighter rock formed the planet's crust. As the crust cooled into solid rock, it cracked into giant plates, called tectonic plates.

By 4.4 billion years ago, Earth had cooled enough for rain, which fell from its atmosphere, to fill oceans in dips in the crust. Earth was now the right temperature—and the right distance from the Sun— for all its water to neither freeze into ice nor boil into steam. It was in the oceans that, around 4 billion years ago, tiny living things appeared.

Even today, Earth's mantle is so hot, up to 3,700 °C (6,690 °F), that some of its rock is molten. Movements of mantle rock cause slow movements of Earth's tectonic plates, which—over millions of years—shift continents, push up mountains, and create volcanoes. Deep inside our planet, the metal

in the outer core is still so hot, over 4,500 °C (8,130 °F), that it is liquid. The inner core is even hotter, around 5,400 °C (9,750 °F)—as hot as the Sun's surface. Yet in the inner core, the metal is squeezed so tightly it is solid.

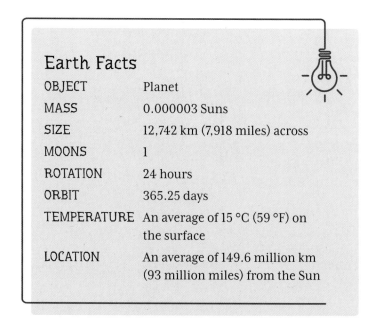

Earth Facts

OBJECT	Planet
MASS	0.000003 Suns
SIZE	12,742 km (7,918 miles) across
MOONS	1
ROTATION	24 hours
ORBIT	365.25 days
TEMPERATURE	An average of 15 °C (59 °F) on the surface
LOCATION	An average of 149.6 million km (93 million miles) from the Sun

Astronomers cannot be sure, but many think the Moon formed when a Mars-sized planet, called Theia, crashed into Earth at around 14,000 km/h (8,700 miles per hour). Pieces of Earth and Theia came together to form the Moon.

Earth's Atmosphere

There would be no life on Earth without its atmosphere, the blanket of gases held around our planet by its gravity. The atmosphere—also known as air, contains the gas oxygen and water. Earth's living things need oxygen and water to survive.

Air is around 78 percent nitrogen and 21 percent oxygen gas, with traces of gases such as argon. Plants and animals need to take in oxygen to make energy for living. Scientists divide the atmosphere into layers, each layer less packed with air than the one below, as the pull of Earth's gravity weakens. The lowest layer, called the troposphere, also holds lots of water, mostly in the form of a gas called water vapor. When this water falls as rain, it gives plants and animals the water needed to transport food through their bodies.

When the Sun's visible light (see page 88) reaches Earth's atmosphere, it is scattered by molecules of gas. Sunlight contains all the shades of the rainbow, from red to blue. Blue light is scattered more than the rest, because it travels as shorter waves. This makes the sky look blue during daytime, even though the gases in the atmosphere are invisible.

MESOSPHERE

This is where streaks of light, known as meteors or shooting stars, can be seen. When fragments from comets and asteroids enter the atmosphere, they crash into air molecules, getting so hot they usually burn up, creating bright streaks. If a rock is large enough to survive and hit the ground, it is called a meteorite.

TROPOSPHERE

As the Sun warms Earth's oceans and lakes, some water evaporates—it turns into water vapor and drifts into the troposphere. As the water vapor cools, some condenses into drops of liquid water, forming clouds. When the drops grow heavy, they fall as rain.

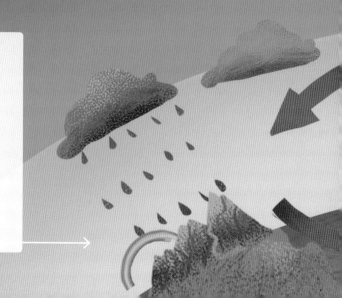

EXOSPHERE

Extending to 10,000 km (6,200 miles) above Earth's surface, this is where many human-made satellites orbit. The exosphere fades gradually into space, where there is almost nothing at all, just a little dust, gas, and high-energy particles from the Sun.

THERMOSPHERE

The thermosphere extends from 80 to 600 km (50 to 370 miles) above the surface. This is the region where auroras form (see page 28).

STRATOSPHERE

The stratosphere lies between 10 and 50 km (6 and 30 miles) above Earth's surface. Passenger planes often fly in the low stratosphere, above the clouds of the troposphere, where the air is relatively still.

Earth's Orbit

Every 365.25 days, Earth completes an orbit around the Sun, having journeyed 940 million km (584 million miles). Like all orbits, Earth's is not a perfect circle, but an oval called an ellipse. When closest to the Sun, Earth is 147 million km (91 million miles) away, while at the farthest it is 152 million km (94 million miles) away.

A YEAR ON EARTH

For thousands of years, humans have devised calendars to mark out the passing of time. Around the world, the most commonly used calendar is based on Earth's orbit around the Sun, with a year equal to one orbit. It is sometimes called the Gregorian calendar because it was introduced by Pope Gregory XIII, in 1582.

In most parts of the world, we can follow the course of Earth's journey around the Sun by watching the changing seasons through the year. Seasons are caused by the fact that Earth's axis is slightly tilted. When the northern hemisphere (half) of Earth is tilted toward the Sun, it has summer with hotter weather. At the same time, the southern hemisphere of Earth has winter, with colder weather. Places close to the equator see fewer seasonal changes, as they are hot all year.

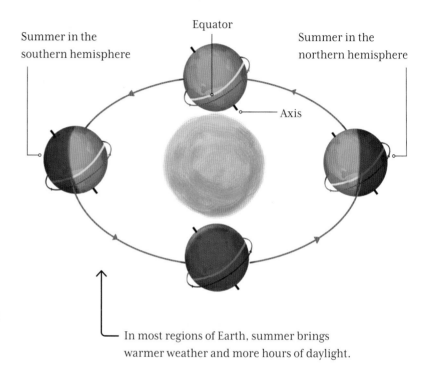

Summer in the southern hemisphere

Equator

Summer in the northern hemisphere

Axis

In most regions of Earth, summer brings warmer weather and more hours of daylight.

Spring

Summer

A DAY ON EARTH

As Earth orbits, it also rotates around its axis. Each rotation takes nearly exactly 24 hours—which we call a day. As Earth turns, the Sun appears to rise in the east, then set in the west. When one half of Earth is turned toward the Sun, it has daylight, while the other half has night.

Due to Earth's tilted axis, days and nights are not usually of equal length. When the northern hemisphere is tilted toward the Sun, it has longer days and shorter nights, while the southern hemisphere has longer nights. The poles see the most extreme pattern of darkness and light. During their winter, the poles are plunged into darkness for around 11 weeks.

CALENDAR CATCH-UP

Since Earth's orbit takes 365.25 days, it is impossible for the calendar—based on days of equal length—to keep pace with it. To correct this problem, we use a system of leap years. Most calendar years have 365 days, but every 4 years, we add an extra day—February 29—so the calendar year again matches up with the astronomical year. This system was introduced by the ancient Roman ruler Julius Caesar in 45 BCE, and was later adjusted by Pope Gregory.

Earth's Orbit Facts

TIME	365.25 days
DIRECTION	Counterclockwise
SPEED	107,208 km/h (66,616 miles per hour) on average
DISTANCE	940 million km (584 million miles) covered in each orbit
APHELION	Farthest distance from the Sun is 152.1 million km (94.5 million miles)
PERIHELION	Closest distance to the Sun is 147.1 million km (91.4 million km)

In Earth's temperate regions, which are midway between the poles and the equator, there are four seasons. The seasons can be observed through the changing temperature, which causes changes in many trees.

Fall or autumn

Winter

Earth's Auroras

Auroras are dancing lights in the sky that can be seen close to the North and South Poles. These beautiful light displays are most easily watched on dark, cloudless nights, far from the disturbance of city lights.

SOLAR WIND

Auroras are caused by the solar wind, a stream of electrically charged particles that flows constantly from the Sun. These particles include electrons, which are far smaller than a billionth of a millimeter across. When these high-energy particles meet Earth's atmosphere, they pass on energy to its gases. The molecules of gas begin to glow, with different gases glowing different shades. Oxygen usually glows green, but higher above Earth's surface, very excited oxygen can give off red light. Nitrogen tends to glow pink or purple.

All the other Solar System planets, apart from Mercury, experience auroras. Mercury has such a thin atmosphere that there are not enough gas molecules to be excited by the solar wind. Auroras have also been seen on the four largest moons of Jupiter, all of which have atmospheres. Auroras on other planets and moons are different shades, since their atmospheres contain different gases. On Saturn, for example, hydrogen glows red and purple.

EARTH'S MAGNETIC FIELD

Auroras can be seen only around Earth's poles because it is here that the planet's magnetic field is weakest. Due to its iron core, Earth is a giant magnet with a powerful magnetic field. Magnetism is a force that can be made by the flow of electrons through magnetic metals, such as iron. As liquid iron swirls in Earth's outer core, electrons flow, creating the magnetic field.

Earth's magnetic field protects it from the solar wind, which would otherwise strip away the atmosphere. Yet some charged particles manage to touch the atmosphere around the poles. Here they can become trapped between magnetic field lines, creating glowing arcs in the night sky. Charged particles can also be scattered into the atmosphere, creating widespread, patchy auroras.

Lines of magnetic force flow from one of Earth's poles to the other. This magnetic field diverts most of the particles of the solar wind.

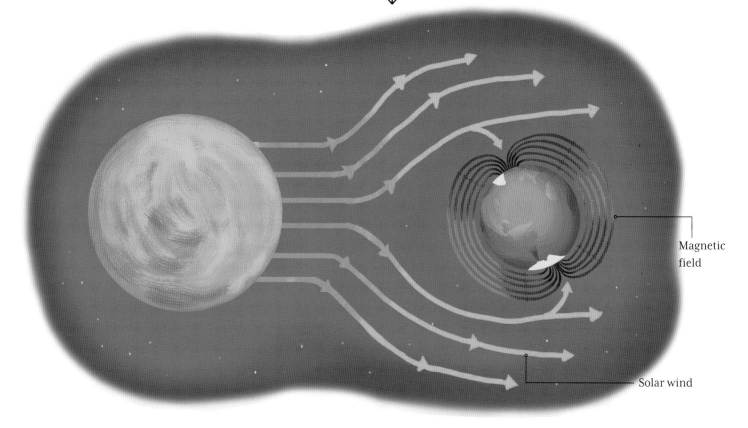

Magnetic field

Solar wind

Auroras can be seen on cloudless winter nights in places such as the far north of Norway, in northern Europe.

The Moon

Earth's Moon is the fifth largest in the Solar System, after three moons of Jupiter and one of Saturn. During its orbit around Earth, the Moon travels as far as 406,700 km (252,700 miles) and as close as 356,400 km (221,500 miles), when it appears 14 percent larger, earning the name "supermoon."

SEAS AND CRATERS

The dark areas that we can see on the Moon are often called seas (*maria* in Latin) because they were once believed to contain water. In fact, these areas are covered in dried lava that flowed from volcanoes billions of years ago. The lava cooled into the dark rock basalt, which is also common on Earth where volcanoes have erupted.

We can also see bright impact craters where asteroids and comets plunged into the Moon, mostly in the early years of the Solar System. The Moon has over 9,000 impact craters. Since the Moon has almost no atmosphere—and therefore no wind and no rain to wear away rock—these craters remain as deep as when they were first made. The largest crater, the South Pole—Aitken Basin, is around 2,500 km (1,600 miles) wide and 4.2 billion years old.

SAME OLD FACE

The Moon takes the same time to orbit Earth as it does to rotate around its axis—27.3 days. All the large moons in the Solar System also have equal orbits and rotations, a feature known as tidal locking.

- Solid metal inner core
- Liquid metal outer core
- Partly melted rock inner mantle
- Solid rock outer mantle
- Solid rock crust

The Moon is made of similar materials to Earth. It has a small metal core, mostly iron with a little nickel, surrounded by a rocky mantle and crust. The crust's most common rocks are basalt and paler anorthosite.

This is because the pull of their planets' gravity slows their rotations to match their orbits.

Due to tidal locking, the Moon always has the same face turned toward Earth. (To understand why, roll a ball around yourself, while turning it so it finishes a rotation and an orbit together.) The face of the Moon that we see from Earth is often called the "near side." The first humans to see the "far side" were the three US astronauts onboard Apollo 8 in 1968.

OCEAN TIDES

Although the Moon's gravity is much weaker than Earth's, its effects can be seen on the world's oceans. The Moon pulls the oceans toward itself, creating bulges that make water rise up the shore, known as high tide. As Earth rotates, the water bulges move around the planet, making the tides rise and fall. When the Moon and Sun are lined up on the same side of Earth, their combined gravity creates extra-high tides.

The Moon Facts

OBJECT	Moon
MASS	0.012 Earths
SIZE	3,476 km (2,160 miles) across
ROTATION	27.3 days
ORBIT	27.3 days
TEMPERATURE	An average of -23 °C (-85 °F) on the surface
LOCATION	An average of 384,402 km (238,856 miles) from Earth

The Moon has too little atmosphere to shield it from the Sun or hold in heat, so its surface ranges from a freezing -173 °C (-279 °F) at night to a boiling 117 °C (242 °F) during the day. With no atmosphere and no liquid water, the Moon is unsuitable for life.

Watching the Moon

If we watch the Moon, it appears to change as it journeys around Earth, while our planet also journeys around the Sun. These apparent changes in the Moon's shape are due to the fact we can only ever see the portion of the Moon that is lit by the Sun.

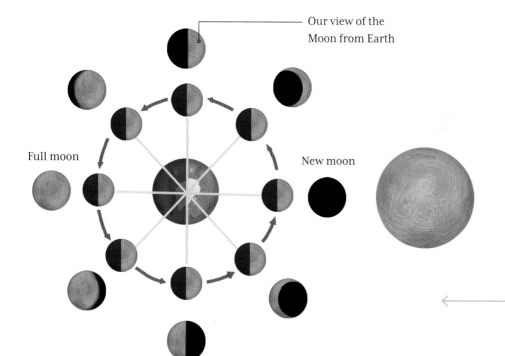

Our view of the
Moon from Earth

Full moon

New moon

PHASES OF THE MOON

As the Moon orbits Earth, it appears to change from a new moon, when none of its face is visible, to a full moon, when we can see its whole near side. New moon is when the Moon lies between the Sun and Earth, so its lit side is not visible to us. Full moon takes place when the Moon is on the opposite side of Earth. Although the Moon's orbit takes 27.3 days, Earth's orbit around the Sun means it takes 29.5 days for the Moon to return to the same position in our sky and move through its phases.

ECLIPSES OF THE MOON

An eclipse of the Moon is when the Moon moves into Earth's shadow. This can happen at full moon if the Sun, Earth, and Moon are lined up. There is not an eclipse at every full moon because the tilts of the Moon's and Earth's orbits mean an exact line-up happens only up to four times a year. A total eclipse is when the Moon is in the central, darkest portion of Earth's shadow, while a penumbral eclipse is when it is in the outer part of the shadow.

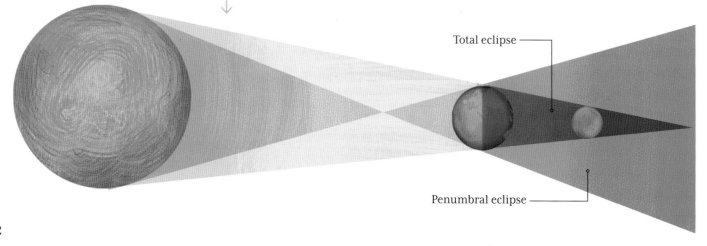

Total eclipse

Penumbral eclipse

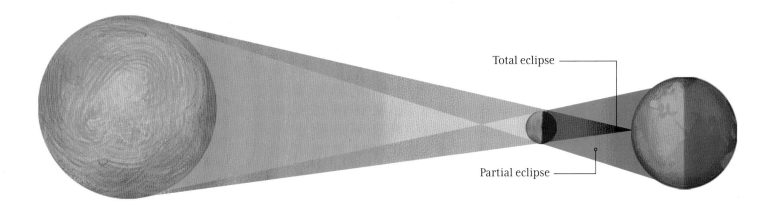

Total eclipse

Partial eclipse

ECLIPSES OF THE SUN

A solar eclipse takes place when, as the Moon passes between the Sun and Earth, it partly or totally blocks the view of our star from a portion of Earth's surface. A total eclipse can be seen from somewhere on Earth around every 18 months, when the Sun, Moon, and Earth are exactly lined up and the Moon is close enough to Earth to fully block the view.

MAPPING THE MOON

People have watched the Moon since ancient times, but the first person to make a detailed map of the Moon's near side was the Polish astronomer Johannes Hevelius, in 1647. He spent several years observing and making measurements of the Moon's surface, using telescopes he built himself.

Mars

The fourth planet is named after the Roman god of war. It gained this name due to its blood-like shade. Mars can be seen as a small red light without the help of a telescope. The planet rotates in around the same time as Earth does, but its orbit takes 322 days longer.

RED PLANET

Mars's redness is caused by the shade of its surface rocks, as well as the large quantities of red dust in its atmosphere. Mars's extreme dustiness is due to the blasting of its rocks by storms and probably—long ago—by water (see page 36). The battering broke some of Mars's rock into fine pieces. The planet's current dryness allows this light dust to be whipped 30 km (19 miles) high by winds of up to 100 km/h (62 miles per hour).

The surface of the Martian rocks is reddish due to containing lots of iron oxide, which is often known as "rust" when it occurs on Earth. Here, rust forms when iron is in contact with oxygen in the air. Mars and Earth formed from similar materials, but while most of Earth's iron sank to its core, much of the Martian iron remained nearer the surface. Although Mars's atmosphere does not currently have enough oxygen to rust the iron in its rocks, it may once have contained more.

Mars Facts	
OBJECT	Planet
MASS	0.107 Earths
SIZE	6,779 km (4,212 miles) across
MOONS	2
ROTATION	1.02 days
ORBIT	687 days
TEMPERATURE	An average of -65 °C (-85 °F) on the surface
LOCATION	An average of 227.9 million km (141.6 million miles) from the Sun

TALLEST VOLCANO

Mars is home to the tallest volcano, which is also the tallest mountain, in the Solar System—Olympus Mons. It is 21.9 km (13.6 miles) tall, more than twice the height of Earth's highest mountain, Mount Everest. The volcano may have started to form over 3 billion years ago on top of an extremely hot area in the mantle, which forced melted rock to the surface. The most recent lava flows are around 115 million years old.

TWO MOONS

The two Martian moons are called Phobos ("fear") and Deimos ("panic"), named after the sons of the Greek god of war, Ares, who followed their father onto the battlefield. Phobos is 22.2 km (13.8 miles) wide, while Deimos is 12.6 km (7.8 miles) across. Both moons are too small to be pulled into a sphere-shape by their own gravity.

Phobos orbits closer to its planet than any other moon—just 9,377 km (5,827 miles) away. Thanks to the pull of Mars's gravity, it is getting closer by around 2 cm (0.8 in) every year—and in around 50 million years will smash into the planet.

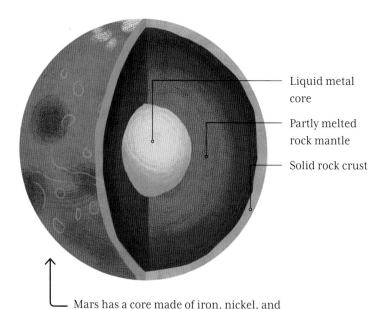

Liquid metal core

Partly melted rock mantle

Solid rock crust

Mars has a core made of iron, nickel, and sulfur, which may be completely liquid. Surrounding this is a rocky mantle up to 1,880 km (1,168 miles) thick, wrapped in an iron-rich rocky crust.

Mars's most visible feature is a series of canyons, the Valles Marineris, that stretch 4,000 km (2,485 miles) across the planet. The canyons cracked as magma pushed up the crust. Mars's moons, Phobos (bottom right) and Deimos (top right), may once have been asteroids orbiting in the Asteroid Belt, but were pulled toward Mars by its gravity.

History of Mars

Today, Mars is dry, cold, and unsuitable for life. Yet the planet was once very different—even Earth-like. No evidence of ancient life has been found on Mars, but long ago, the planet was warm and watery enough to be suitable for living things.

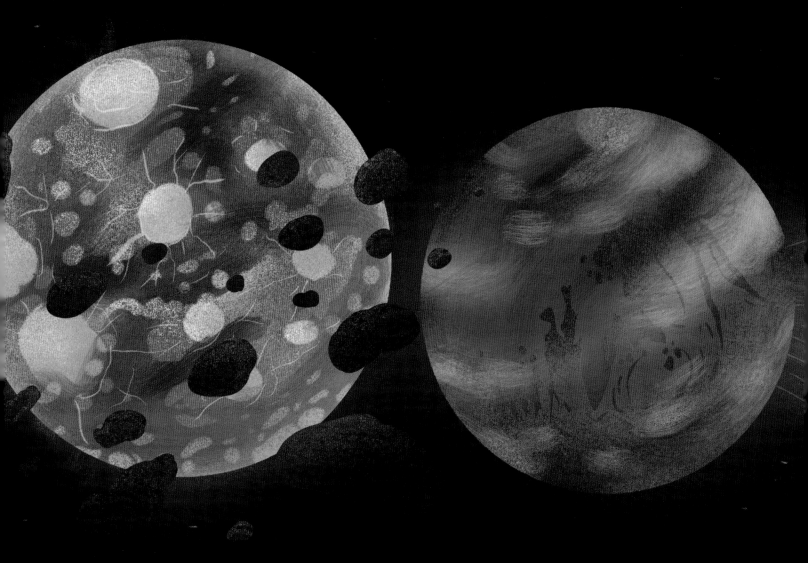

4.5 BILLION YEARS AGO

Mars formed at the same time as Earth. Over the next few million years, the young Mars's volcanoes spewed out gases, creating a thick atmosphere held by the planet's gravity. Due to the churning iron in its core, Mars had a magnetic field that protected the atmosphere from being blown away by the solar wind (see page 28).

4 BILLION YEARS AGO

Clouds of water droplets floated though Mars's atmosphere. Rain filled the lakes and oceans, which covered one-third of the planet's surface. Today, evidence of oceans and rivers can be seen in the rocks that they wore away, and the sand they carried.

On Earth, life is possible because we have liquid water and an oxygen-rich atmosphere. Mars's dryness and thin atmosphere make life extremely unlikely there today. Yet astronomers believe that, billions of years ago, Mars had oceans and rivers. It also had a thick atmosphere, although we are not sure if it was as oxygen-filled as Earth's.

Mars's past suitability for life does not necessarily mean that life did exist there. However, astronomers wonder if the planet might have been home to tiny living things, such as bacteria. Such simple living things were the earliest life forms on Earth. If tiny living things did once exist—or even still exist—evidence might be found deep in the Martian soil. Armed with drills, rovers search Mars constantly for that evidence.

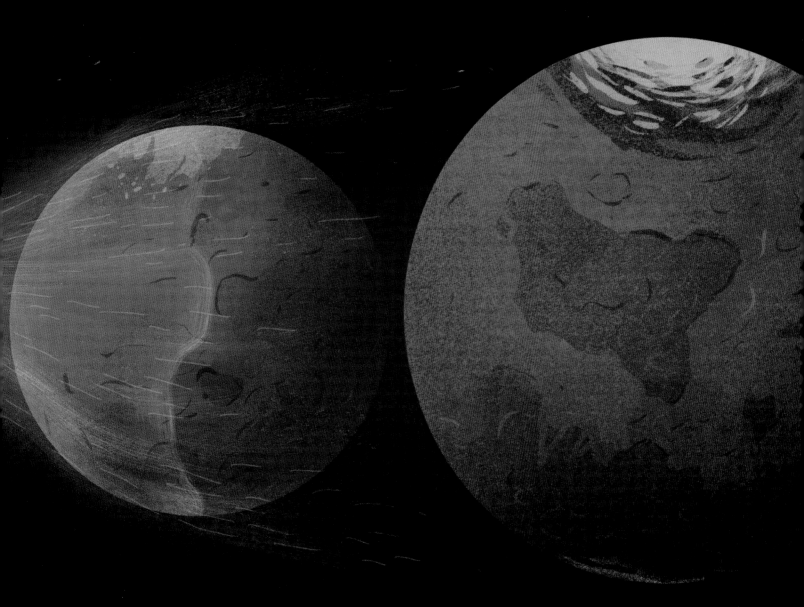

3.7 BILLION YEARS AGO

The churning of Mars's core slowed, possibly due to cooling or a series of asteroid strikes. The planet lost its magnetic field. All but 1 percent of the atmosphere was stripped away by the solar wind. With so little atmosphere to press down on it, the planet's liquid water drifted off into space or froze into ice.

TODAY

With no warming blanket of atmosphere, the temperature on Mars drops to -153 °C (-243 °F) at the poles. There is still enough water to cover the planet in an ocean 35 m (115 ft) deep. Yet all this water is frozen in the soil and at the poles, which are capped by sheets of ice around 1,000 km (620 miles) across.

The Asteroid Belt

Between the orbits of Mars and Jupiter, millions of asteroids are circling the Sun. Like the inner planets, asteroids are made mostly of rock and metal. The largest of the asteroids, called Ceres, is big enough to be considered a dwarf planet.

MAKING THE BELT

The Asteroid Belt contains material that was left over during the formation of the Solar System. The immense gravity of Jupiter stopped this material from clumping together into a planet. Instead, the differently sized and shaped chunks orbit in a ring-shaped region between 329 million and 479 million km (204 million and 298 million miles) from the Sun.

The mass of all the material in the Asteroid Belt is only 0.5 percent of Earth's mass. The four largest asteroids—Ceres, Vesta, Pallas, and Hygeia—make up more than half the Belt's mass. To be called an asteroid, an object has to be at least 1 m (3.3 ft) across, although plenty of smaller objects and dust also orbit in the Asteroid Belt. Up to 1.7 million asteroids are wider than 1 km (0.6 miles).

Despite their small size, more than 300 asteroids are known to have moons. These moons were probably made by collisions, which broke off fragments that stayed close to their parent asteroid. Just 200 km (124 miles) wide, Elektra has the most known moons of any asteroid—three.

WATERY CERES

At around 939 km (583 miles) wide, Ceres has powerful enough gravity to have pulled itself into a rough sphere, earning itself the title of "dwarf planet." It is the only agreed dwarf planet that orbits entirely inside the orbit of Neptune.

Ceres is rocky, but it is also approximately half water. This makes it one of the most watery objects in the Solar System, a little less watery than Earth. Much of Ceres's water is mixed with rock, forming mud or clay. However, astronomers think the dwarf planet may have pockets of salty water beneath its surface. This water could possibly be home to tiny life forms, but no space probe has yet landed on Ceres to find out.

Ceres has a large ice volcano, known as a cryovolcano, as well as the remains of several others. None of Ceres's cryovolcanoes is currently active, but they once erupted icy, muddy water. These eruptions were possibly caused by collisions with other asteroids, which melted icy material and broke the crust.

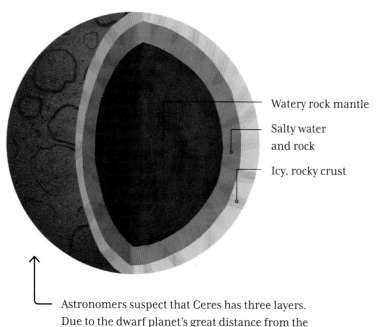

Watery rock mantle

Salty water and rock

Icy, rocky crust

Astronomers suspect that Ceres has three layers. Due to the dwarf planet's great distance from the Sun, its surface is frozen.

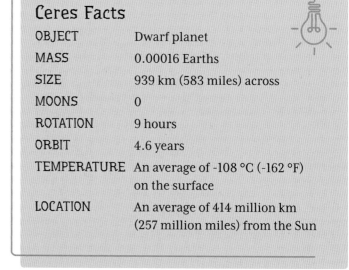

Ceres Facts

OBJECT	Dwarf planet
MASS	0.00016 Earths
SIZE	939 km (583 miles) across
MOONS	0
ROTATION	9 hours
ORBIT	4.6 years
TEMPERATURE	An average of -108 °C (-162 °F) on the surface
LOCATION	An average of 414 million km (257 million miles) from the Sun

On average, there are around 100,000 km (62,000 miles) between any two asteroids in the Asteroid Belt. However, collisions between asteroids occur every few million years. Fast collisions shatter asteroids, while slower crashes may join them.

Jupiter

The largest planet is named after the king of the Roman gods. Like its sister planet Saturn, Jupiter is a gas giant, made mostly of hydrogen and helium. It has the largest ocean in the Solar System, but it is an ocean of hydrogen and helium rather than water.

GAS GIANT

Jupiter and Saturn are called gas giants because hydrogen and helium are gasses at room temperature on Earth. Yet on these planets, hydrogen and helium take different forms—gas, liquid, and metallic. Jupiter's atmosphere is mostly hydrogen and helium gas. The atmosphere mingles with the planet's interior, where the gas is so tightly squeezed that it becomes liquid. Deeper inside the planet, electrons are squeezed out of the hydrogen and helium atoms. This means that electricity starts to flow, as if the swirling fluid were a metal.

Jupiter has no solid surface on which a spacecraft could land. The only solid portion of Jupiter is its core, which is probably iron and rock with a temperature of 24,000 °C (43,000 °F). However a spacecraft flying into Jupiter would be destroyed by pressure and heat long before it reached the core.

Jupiter's faint rings were not discovered until 1979, when they were spotted by the *Voyager 1* space probe. They are made of orbiting dust that was thrown from the planet's moons.

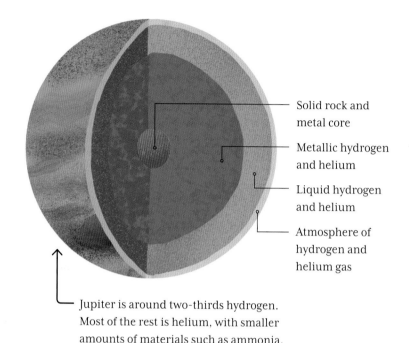

Solid rock and metal core

Metallic hydrogen and helium

Liquid hydrogen and helium

Atmosphere of hydrogen and helium gas

Jupiter is around two-thirds hydrogen. Most of the rest is helium, with smaller amounts of materials such as ammonia.

Jupiter Facts

OBJECT	Planet
MASS	318 Earths
SIZE	142,984 km (88,846 miles) across
MOONS	95 known
ROTATION	10 hours
ORBIT	11.9 years
TEMPERATURE	An average of -110 °C (-166 °F) on the surface
LOCATION	An average of 778.5 million km (483.7 million miles) from the Sun

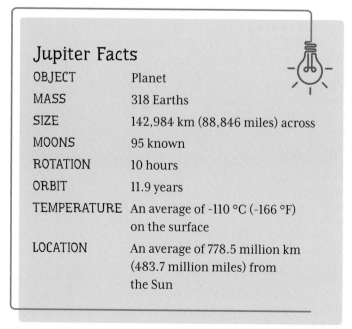

SPEEDY SPINNER

Jupiter spins around its axis faster than any other Solar System planet, at around 45,000 km/h (28,000 miles per hour). This speedy spin makes the planet bulge at the equator, a little like how a ball of dough starts to flatten into a pizza when spun. Jupiter is 9,276 km (5,764 miles) wider across its equator than across its poles.

Jupiter's fast spin creates powerful winds, which blow east to west and west to east in alternating bands. These winds separate Jupiter's clouds—which are made of materials such as ammonia—into horizontal stripes.

The orange stripes, called belts, are regions of cool, sinking gas that has been stained by sunlight. The light stripes, called zones, are warmer, rising gas.

Where belts and zones meet, circling storms can form. The largest storm, called the Great Red Spot, is around 16,000 km (9,940 miles) across—wider than Earth. Its winds spiral at up to 432 km/h (268 miles per hour). The storm has been observed by astronomers since at least 1831, when it was even larger than it is today.

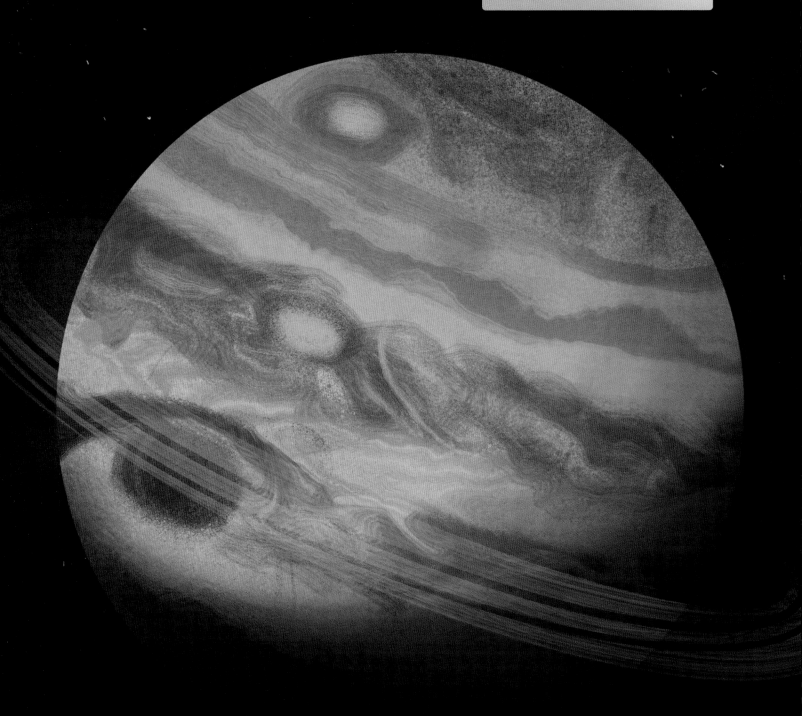

The Great Red Spot can be seen around 25,000 km (15,500 miles) south of Jupiter's equator. Although the storm is usually red, it has been known to change to orange, salmon, and beige.

Jupiter's Moons

Jupiter has 95 known moons, not including its moonlets, around 1 m (3.3 ft) across, and possibly hundreds of small moons that orbit many millions of kilometers away. The four largest moons—Ganymede, Callisto, Io, and Europa—were discovered by Galileo Galilei in 1610.

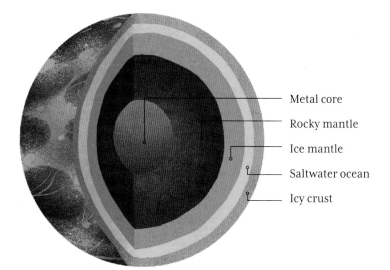

Metal core
Rocky mantle
Ice mantle
Saltwater ocean
Icy crust

GANYMEDE

The Solar System's largest moon, Ganymede, formed soon after Jupiter, from the gas and dust spinning around its parent planet. Beneath its icy crust, the moon has a saltwater ocean, which could possibly be home to tiny life forms.

CALLISTO

At 4,820 km (2,995 miles) wide, Jupiter's second largest moon is the Solar System's third largest, after Saturn's moon Titan. Callisto is one of the most cratered objects in the Solar System, with hundreds of impact craters up to 1,800 km (1,120 miles) wide.

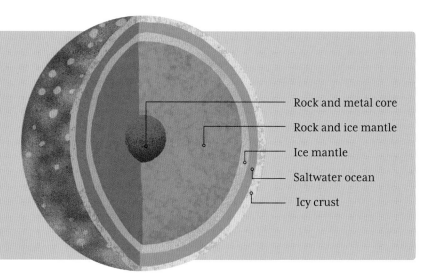

Rock and metal core
Rock and ice mantle
Ice mantle
Saltwater ocean
Icy crust

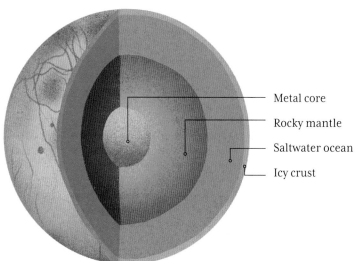

Metal core
Rocky mantle
Saltwater ocean
Icy crust

EUROPA

The smallest of the four moons discovered by Galileo, Europa is 3,122 km (1,940 miles) wide. It has a strangely uncratered surface, which suggests that a deep, warm ocean beneath the icy crust allows it to spring back into shape when struck. Long cracks in the crust may be caused by water welling up.

Ganymede Facts

OBJECT	Moon
MASS	0.025 Earths
SIZE	5,268 km (3,273 miles) across
ROTATION	7 days
ORBIT	7 days around Jupiter
TEMPERATURE	An average of -163 °C (-261 °F) on the surface
LOCATION	An average of 1,070,400 km (665,116 miles) from Jupiter

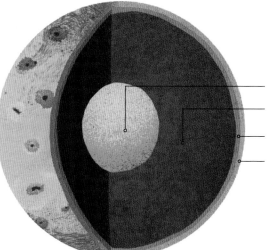

Metal core

Rocky mantle

Ocean of melted rock

Rock and sulfur crust

IO

Io is much closer to Jupiter than the other Galilean moons, around 421,700 km (262,032 miles) from the planet. This has made it hotter and less icy. It is made mostly of iron and rock. Like its sister moons, it is named after a lover of Zeus, the Greek counterpart of Jupiter.

IO'S VOLCANOES

Io has more active volcanoes—around 400—than any other object in the Solar System. The moon is stretched and squeezed by a tug of war between Jupiter's gravity and the gravity of the other Galilean moons. This causes friction in Io's interior, making its rock melt and burst from the surface.

GALILEO GALILEI

When the Italian astronomer Galileo Galilei heard about the invention of the telescope by spectacle-maker Hans Lippershey, he set about making his own. He immediately turned his telescope to the sky, becoming the first person to see a moon orbiting an object other than Earth. The four moons he spotted are called the Galilean moons.

Saturn

The sixth planet from the Sun can be seen as a yellowish point of light in the night sky during most of the year. More than nine times wider than Earth, Saturn is the second biggest planet. It is named after the Roman god of time, wealth, and farming.

DIFFERENT SISTER

Despite its similar materials to Jupiter, Saturn's atmosphere does not display the bright stripes of its sister gas giant. Saturn's stripes are fainter and paler. This is because Saturn's distance from the Sun—and its smaller size, which gives it less inner heat—makes its atmosphere cooler. The upper atmosphere is filled with crystals of frozen ammonia, which give Saturn a more even—and yellowish—appearance.

Saturn is also a lot less dense than Jupiter, which means its atoms and molecules are less tightly packed together. Although Saturn's core is dense, its average overall density is much less dense than water. This means that—if there were a swimming pool big enough to hold Saturn—it would float, for the same reason that a rubber ring floats in water.

HOT INSIDE

Saturn's core is as hot as 11,700 °C (21,000 °F). Due to its huge size, the planet grew massively hot during its formation, because of the crashing of material. Although Saturn has since cooled, plenty of heat remains. Like the other giant planets, it gives off more heat than it receives from the Sun. In fact,

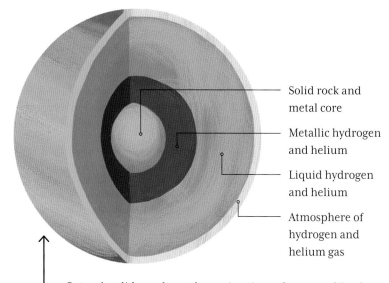

Solid rock and metal core

Metallic hydrogen and helium

Liquid hydrogen and helium

Atmosphere of hydrogen and helium gas

Saturn's solid core has at least nine times the mass of Earth. The rest of Saturn is around three-quarters hydrogen and one-quarter helium, with traces of other materials.

Saturn gives off twice the heat it receives. Due to its vast distance, Saturn gets 1 percent as much sunlight as Earth.

DIAMOND THUNDERSTORMS

Once every orbit, which takes 29.5 years, white streaks can be seen wrapping around Saturn's northern hemisphere for a few weeks. Known as the Great White Spot, these streaks are thunderstorms caused by rapidly rising, hot gas. On Earth, quickly rising, hot, wet air also causes thunderstorms. When lightning in Saturn's storms strikes methane in the atmosphere, it turns to carbon. The carbon hardens into diamonds as it falls—creating diamond rain.

Saturn's thunderstorms happen when its northern hemisphere is most tilted toward the Sun. Like all the planets except Mercury, which is almost upright, Saturn's axis is tilted. While Earth's axis tilts by around 23 degrees (see page 26), Saturn's tilts a little more, by nearly 27 degrees. Astronomers think that all the planets were upright when they formed, but were tipped by crashes with asteroids.

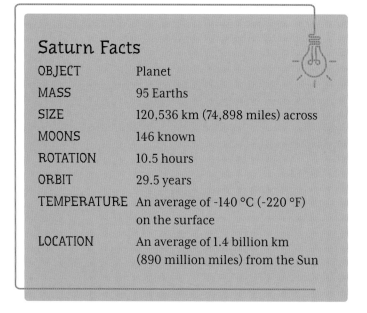

Saturn Facts

OBJECT	Planet
MASS	95 Earths
SIZE	120,536 km (74,898 miles) across
MOONS	146 known
ROTATION	10.5 hours
ORBIT	29.5 years
TEMPERATURE	An average of -140 °C (-220 °F) on the surface
LOCATION	An average of 1.4 billion km (890 million miles) from the Sun

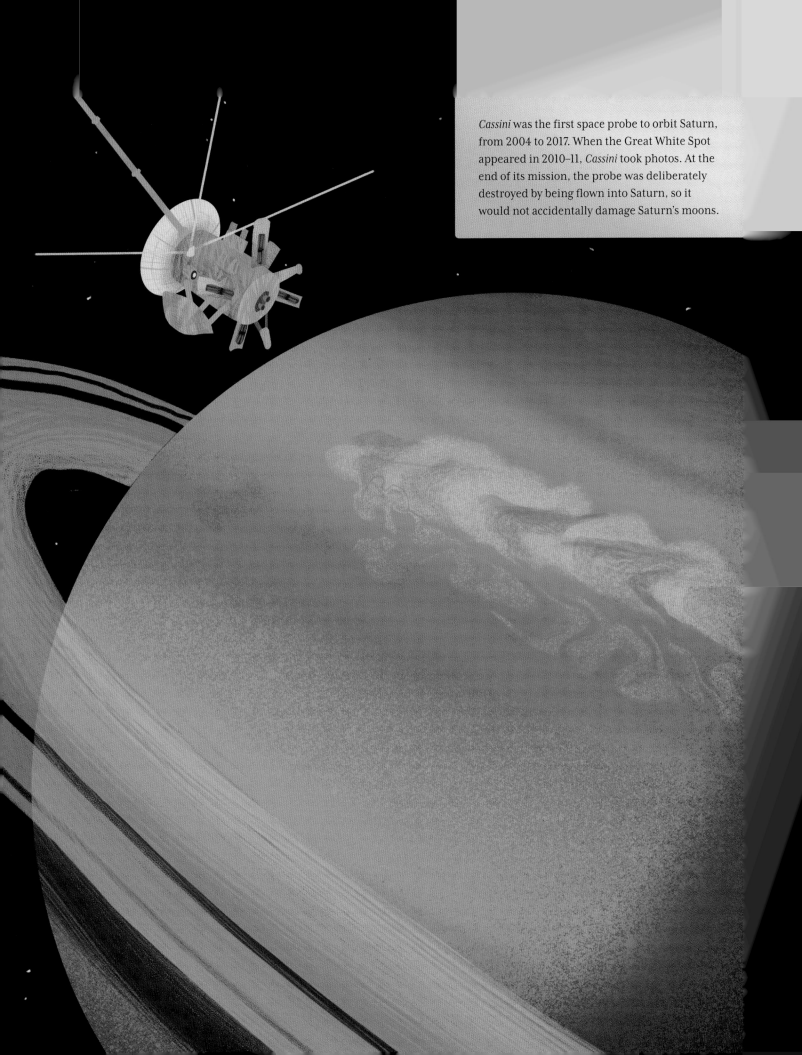

Cassini was the first space probe to orbit Saturn, from 2004 to 2017. When the Great White Spot appeared in 2010–11, *Cassini* took photos. At the end of its mission, the probe was deliberately destroyed by being flown into Saturn, so it would not accidentally damage Saturn's moons.

Saturn's Rings

Saturn has the Solar System's brightest and largest ring system, stretching 400,000 km (248,000 miles) from the planet's surface. The rings are made mostly of chunks of ice, which orbit the planet around its equator. The rings' brightness is due to their iciness, which makes them reflect sunlight.

The rings may have formed less than 100 million years ago, when one of Saturn's moons was shattered by an asteroid, or perhaps when a comet was torn apart by the planet's gravity. The chunks of moon or comet were held in orbit by Saturn's gravity. Slowly, the jumbled rubble shifted into rings, divided by gaps where Saturn's moons and tinier moonlets pulled away much of the material.

Saturn's main, most densely packed rings are named A, B, and C. Visible from Earth only through a telescope, the rings were named in the order they were seen. A and B were first seen blurrily by Italian astronomer Galileo Galilei in 1610, through his newly built telescope. The C ring was spotted in 1850. Inside and far beyond these main rings are fainter rings that were discovered with powerful modern telescopes, or by space probes.

A RING

This ring stretches between 63,940 and 78,540 km (39,730 and 48,800 miles) from Saturn's surface. It is 10 to 30 m (33 to 98 ft) thick. Most of its chunks are smaller than 10 m (33 ft) across, but together they weigh many trillions of kilograms—around 0.000003 Earth masses.

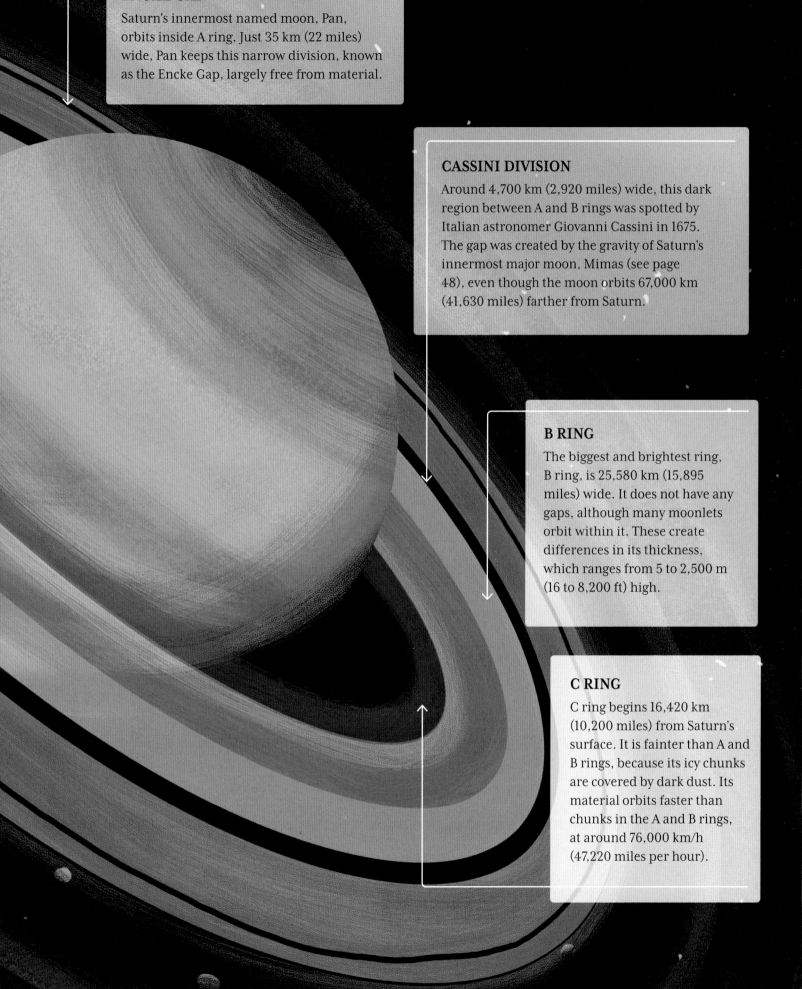

Saturn's innermost named moon, Pan, orbits inside A ring. Just 35 km (22 miles) wide, Pan keeps this narrow division, known as the Encke Gap, largely free from material.

CASSINI DIVISION

Around 4,700 km (2,920 miles) wide, this dark region between A and B rings was spotted by Italian astronomer Giovanni Cassini in 1675. The gap was created by the gravity of Saturn's innermost major moon, Mimas (see page 48), even though the moon orbits 67,000 km (41,630 miles) farther from Saturn.

B RING

The biggest and brightest ring, B ring, is 25,580 km (15,895 miles) wide. It does not have any gaps, although many moonlets orbit within it. These create differences in its thickness, which ranges from 5 to 2,500 m (16 to 8,200 ft) high.

C RING

C ring begins 16,420 km (10,200 miles) from Saturn's surface. It is fainter than A and B rings, because its icy chunks are covered by dark dust. Its material orbits faster than chunks in the A and B rings, at around 76,000 km/h (47,220 miles per hour).

Saturn's immense gravity allows it to hold on to at least 140 moons, as well as countless smaller moonlets. The planet's largest moon, Titan, is the Solar System's second largest moon. Titan is also one of the most likely places in the Solar System to be home to life.

THE BIG SEVEN

Saturn's smallest known moons are oddly shaped icy rocks around 1 km (0.6 miles) across, while the planet's many moonlets are smaller still. Seven of Saturn's moons are large enough that their gravity has pulled them into a rounded shape. From largest to smallest, these moons are: Titan, Rhea, Iapetus, Dione, Tethys, Enceladus, and Mimas.

Mimas is the closest major moon to Saturn, at 185,539 km (115,289 miles) from the planet's core. Just 396 km (246 miles) wide, it is the smallest known space object that has pulled itself into a ball. The farthest major moon from Saturn is Iapetus, 3.6 million km (2.2 million miles) away. Yet this is not Saturn's outermost moon, which is at least 26 million km (16 million miles) away. Both Mimas and Iapetus are mostly frozen water, mixed with rock.

Mimas · Enceladus · Tethys · Dione · Rhea · Titan · Iapetus

Saturn's major moons are shown in order of their distance from the planet. Titan is bigger than the planet Mercury, but has less than half its mass, as the moon contains lots of ice, which is less "heavy" than rock and metal.

Titan has the thickest atmosphere of any known moon. Unlike Earth's atmosphere, Titan's does not contain oxygen—it is mainly nitrogen gas, which also makes up much of Earth's atmosphere. Titan is also the only object in the Solar System, apart from Earth, known to have seas and rivers on its surface. These are not filled with water, but with methane and ethane. However, like water on Earth, these liquids evaporate into gas, then fall back to the surface as rain (see pages 24–25). On Earth, we breathe oxygen and drink water to live. If life forms did exist on Titan's surface, they might breathe nitrogen and drink methane, which would make them completely different from any living thing we know!

Beneath Titan's crust, astronomers think there is an underground ocean of true water. Since life on Earth began in the oceans, there might be life forms here.

This means that Titan has two chances of being home to life—life as we know it below the surface, and, on the surface, life as we absolutely do not know it! So far, only one space probe has landed on Titan, *Huygens* in 2005 (see page 109). It did not find evidence of life—but, one day, more probes will visit.

Titan Facts

OBJECT	Moon
MASS	0.023 Earths
SIZE	5,149 km (3,200 miles) across
ROTATION	15.9 days
ORBIT	15.9 days around Saturn
TEMPERATURE	An average of -179 °C (-290 °F) on the surface
LOCATION	An average of 1,221,870 km (759,235 miles) from Saturn

Titan's vast distance from the Sun makes its surface cold, around -179 °C (-290 °F). The moon's methane and ethane seas are liquid even at this low temperature, but the rest of the surface is covered by frozen water.

Uranus

The seventh planet from the Sun was named after the Greek god of the sky, while most of its 27 known moons were named after characters in the works of the English playwright William Shakespeare. The planet also has a faint ring system, made of ice and dark dust.

ICE GIANT

Uranus and its sister planet Neptune are known as ice giants. Yet they are not made of ice, but mostly of flowing water, ammonia, and methane. Scientists call these materials "ices" because they have freezing points above -273 °C (-459 °F). For example, water's freezing point is 0 °C (32 °F). Below this temperature it is ice. The interior of Uranus is so hot, up to 4,700 °C (8,490 °F) at the rocky core, that most of its "ices" form a super-hot ocean.

Due to its immense distance from the Sun, Uranus takes 84 years to make one orbit. The planet orbits the Sun on its side, with its ring system pointing nearly directly "upward," probably because it was knocked over by a collision with another planet when it was very young.

Due to this strange orientation, each of the planet's poles has nearly 42 years of sunlight when it faces the Sun, followed by almost 42 years of darkness.

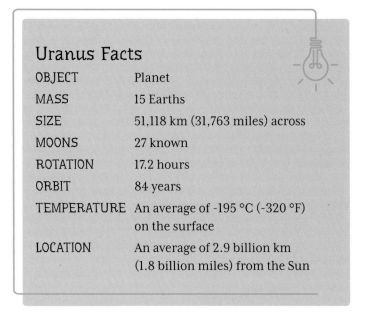

Uranus Facts

OBJECT	Planet
MASS	15 Earths
SIZE	51,118 km (31,763 miles) across
MOONS	27 known
ROTATION	17.2 hours
ORBIT	84 years
TEMPERATURE	An average of -195 °C (-320 °F) on the surface
LOCATION	An average of 2.9 billion km (1.8 billion miles) from the Sun

MANY MOONS

Uranus's largest moon, called Titania, is the eighth largest moon in the Solar System, after Neptune's moon Triton at number seven. Yet the combined mass of all 27 of Uranus's moons is less than the mass of Triton. Around 1,577 km (980 miles) across, Titania is named after the queen of the fairies in Shakespeare's comedy *A Midsummer Night's Dream*. Titania has a rocky core surrounded by frozen water.

Titania is one of Uranus's five large, rounded moons. These orbit between 129,390 and 583,520 km (80,400 and 362,580 miles) from Uranus. The five moons formed at the same time as Uranus from its leftover material.

Orbiting closer to Uranus, within 100,000 km (62,000 miles) of the planet, are 13 small, irregularly shaped moons. They probably formed at the same time as the planet's rings, perhaps when a larger moon was shattered by an asteroid.

Much farther from the planet, up to 20 million km (12.4 million miles) away, are at least nine more small moons. These were probably passing objects captured by Uranus's gravity.

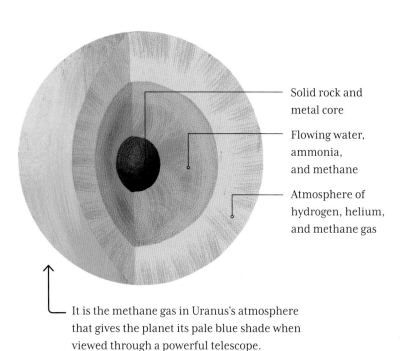

Solid rock and metal core

Flowing water, ammonia, and methane

Atmosphere of hydrogen, helium, and methane gas

It is the methane gas in Uranus's atmosphere that gives the planet its pale blue shade when viewed through a powerful telescope.

Uranus and its largest moon, Titania, can be seen from the icy surface of Oberon. Oberon is the second largest and most distant of the planet's five major moons. It is named after the king of the fairies in Shakespeare's *A Midsummer Night's Dream*.

Neptune

The eighth planet is bluer than its sister ice giant, Uranus. The two planets have similar materials, but Neptune's less-hazy atmosphere makes its shade deeper. Neptune was named after the Roman god of the sea, while its 14 known moons take the names of Greek gods and spirits of water.

DIFFICULT TO FIND

Too distant to be seen with the naked eye, Neptune was found through the teamwork of astronomers and mathematicians. In the early 19th century, French astronomer Alexis Bouvard decided that the gravity of an undiscovered outer planet must be pulling on Uranus, affecting its orbit. French mathematician Urbain Le Verrier calculated where the new planet must be. Finally, German astronomer Johann Galle used this calculation to spot the eighth planet through a telescope, in 1846.

Solid rock and metal core

Flowing water, ammonia, and methane

Atmosphere of hydrogen, helium, and methane gas

Neptune has a similar structure to Uranus. However, its greater mass makes it slightly smaller, as its greater gravity compresses (squeezes) its materials.

WINDIEST PLANET

Neptune has the fastest winds in the Solar System—up to 2,200 km/h (1,367 miles per hour). These are caused by the planet's intense inner heat, 5,100 °C (9,210 °F) at the core, combined with its distance from the Sun, which makes its upper atmosphere around -214 °C (-353 °F). As on Earth, Neptune's winds are movements of gas in the atmosphere. Hot gas rises (like hot water rising in a saucepan), forcing cold gas to sink. Neptune's huge differences in temperature result in high-speed winds and vast storms. The largest storm seen on Neptune, the Great Dark Spot, was 13,000 km (8,000 miles) across.

STRANGE MOONS

Around 2,710 km (1,680 miles) wide, Neptune's largest moon, Triton, is the seventh largest Solar System moon, after four of Jupiter's moons, one of Saturn's, and Earth's Moon. Triton is the only one of Neptune's moons large enough for its gravity to pull it into a rounded shape. The next largest moon, Proteus, is only 420 km (260 miles) across. The most distant known moon, Neso, orbits up to 77 million km (47.8 million km) from Neptune, farther from its parent planet than any other known moon.

Unlike other large moons, Triton orbits its planet in the opposite direction from the way Neptune is rotating—clockwise rather than counterclockwise. This means that Triton cannot have formed at the same time, nor from the same spinning clump of gas and dust as Neptune. The moon may once have been a dwarf planet in the Kuiper Belt, but was pulled by Neptune's gravity. Triton has an almost identical structure to the largest Kuiper Belt dwarf planet—Pluto (see page 54).

Neptune Facts

OBJECT	Planet
MASS	17 Earths
SIZE	49,528 km (30,775 miles) across
MOONS	14 known
ROTATION	16 hours
ORBIT	164.8 years
TEMPERATURE	An average of -201 °C (-330 °F) on the surface
LOCATION	An average of 4.5 billion km (2.8 billion miles) from the Sun

Neptune's biggest moon, Triton, makes up more than 99 percent of the mass of all the objects orbiting the planet, including its rings. There are five main rings, made of dusty ice.

The Kuiper Belt

Named after Dutch astronomer Gerard Kuiper, the Kuiper Belt is a ring of objects between 4.5 billion and 7.5 billion km (2.8 billion and 4.7 billion miles) from the Sun. As the Solar System formed, Neptune's gravity stopped these rocky, icy objects from grouping into a true planet. Yet at least five of the largest objects are big enough to be called dwarf planets.

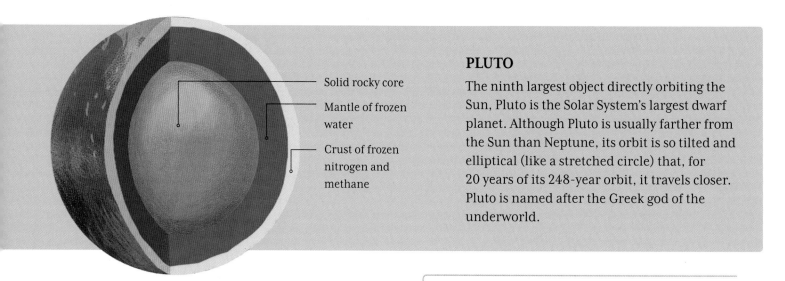

Solid rocky core

Mantle of frozen water

Crust of frozen nitrogen and methane

PLUTO

The ninth largest object directly orbiting the Sun, Pluto is the Solar System's largest dwarf planet. Although Pluto is usually farther from the Sun than Neptune, its orbit is so tilted and elliptical (like a stretched circle) that, for 20 years of its 248-year orbit, it travels closer. Pluto is named after the Greek god of the underworld.

Pluto Facts

OBJECT	Dwarf planet
MASS	0.002 Earths
SIZE	2,376 km (1,476 miles) across
MOONS	5 known
ROTATION	6.4 days
ORBIT	248 years
TEMPERATURE	An average of -229 °C (-380 °F) on the surface
LOCATION	An average of 5.9 billion km (3.7 billion miles) from the Sun

PLUTO'S MOONS

Pluto's five known moons are named after characters and things linked with the underworld of Greek myths. At 1,212 km (753 miles) wide, Charon is the largest moon. It is so big compared with Pluto that both objects orbit a point in space a little outside of Pluto, where the pulls of their gravities are balanced.

Pluto

Charon

Styx

Nix

Hydra

Kerberos

HAUMEA

Up to 2,100 km (1,300 miles) long, Haumea is the second largest Kuiper Belt object. Unlike other dwarf planets, it is not even close to being a sphere. Its gravity pulled it into a rounded shape, but it was flattened by its speedy rotation of 1,600 km/h (995 miles per hour). Haumea has two known moons and a ring system.

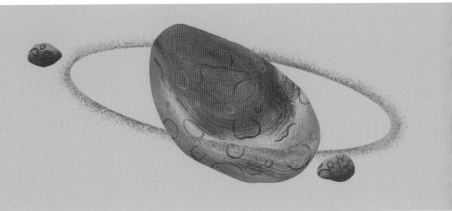

MAKEMAKE

This dwarf planet was named after a creator god of the Pacific Ocean's Rapa Nui people. It has a red surface, like parts of Pluto, caused by sunlight heating methane in its crust. Makemake is about 1,430 km (890 miles) wide and has one known moon.

QUAOAR

Around 1,110 km (690 miles) wide, Quaoar was spotted in 2002 using a big telescope at the Palomar Observatory in California, USA. The dwarf planet was named after the creator god of California's Tongva people, while its moon, Weywot, was named after Quaoar's son.

ORCUS

Orcus was named after the Roman god who punished the dead if they had broken promises. It has one known moon, Vanth, named after a winged spirit who guided souls to the underworld. About 910 km (570 miles) wide, this dwarf planet was discovered in 2004.

Comets

**Comets are icy objects with orbits that take them both far from and close to the Sun.
When near the Sun, comets get so hot they grow glowing tails of gas and dust,
which are sometimes so bright they can be seen without a telescope.**

CREATING COMETS

One of the most famous comets is Halley's Comet, named after the English astronomer Edmond Halley, who was the first to conclude that the bright objects seen in the sky in 1531, 1607, and 1682 were the same comet. The word "comet" comes from the ancient Greek word for "long-haired," referring to these objects' long, glowing tails.

Comets probably started their lives with a regular orbit somewhere in the Kuiper Belt (see page 54), Scattered Disk, or Oort Cloud (see page 58). However, they were disturbed by the gravity of the outer planets or a star, flinging them into extremely elliptical (like stretched circles) orbits around the Sun—and making them comets.

At their closest approach to the Sun, comets may be a few million kilometers away. Some even crash into the Sun and are destroyed. At their most distant, some comets journey trillions of kilometers from the Sun. Comets with shorter orbits, known as short-period comets, have orbits lasting between 3 and 199 years. Long-period comets have orbits of 200 to thousands of years. There are about 4,000 known comets, but there are probably many more currently too far away to be spotted.

In 1066, Halley's Comet passed within 14.5 million km (9 million miles) of Earth. In England, the comet was seen as an omen, a sign of important events. A few weeks later, England's King Harold was beaten in battle by Normandy's William the Conqueror, who took the throne.

LIGHTING UP

A comet is made mostly of frozen water, dust, and rock. This solid core is known as its nucleus. When a comet is in the distant Solar System, it is cool and dark. Yet, as it passes the orbit of Jupiter, a comet heats up enough to release a cloud of gas, known as a coma. As a comet reaches Earth's orbit, a tail of hot gas starts to grow. Then, as the comet nears the Sun, a second tail appears, made of dust from the nucleus.

Eventually, after thousands or millions of years, a comet runs out of gas and dust, so it can no longer release glowing tails. It becomes "extinct," just a small, dark lump of rock.

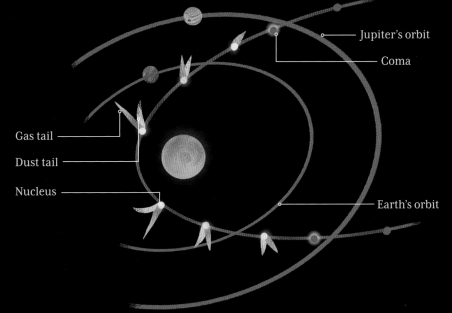

Jupiter's orbit

Coma

Gas tail

Dust tail

Nucleus

Earth's orbit

A comet's gas tail glows blue and is always blown away from the Sun. It may stretch for 150 million km (93 million km). The dust tail is golden and curves toward the path of the comet's orbit.

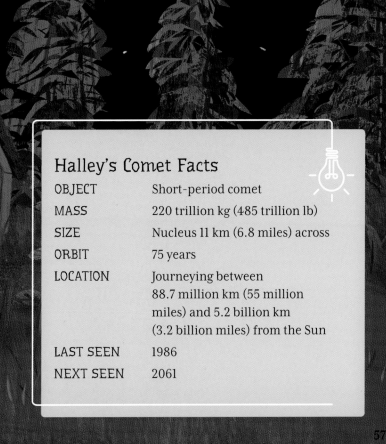

Halley's Comet Facts

OBJECT	Short-period comet
MASS	220 trillion kg (485 trillion lb)
SIZE	Nucleus 11 km (6.8 miles) across
ORBIT	75 years
LOCATION	Journeying between 88.7 million km (55 million miles) and 5.2 billion km (3.2 billion miles) from the Sun
LAST SEEN	1986
NEXT SEEN	2061

Edge of the Solar System

The Kuiper Belt is not the edge of the Solar System. Stretching beyond it is another region of spinning icy objects— the Scattered Disk. Yet even this cold, dark region is not yet the end. Billions of kilometers away are other mysterious objects held by our star's gravity.

Although trillions of objects orbit the Sun beyond Neptune, they are so far from us that not one of them was discovered until powerful telescopes were built in the 20th century. The first object discovered in this vast region was the Kuiper Belt's Pluto, in 1930. It was 66 years later, in 1996, that the first object in the Scattered Disk was seen, using telescopes at Hawaii's Mauna Kea Observatory.

Beyond the Scattered Disk are the detached objects, the first of them found in 2000. Detached objects are too far away to be pulled by the gravity of Neptune, making them seem "detached" from the rest of the Solar System, even though they still orbit the Sun. No one has yet spotted an object in the even more distant Oort Cloud. In fact, we do not know for sure that it exists. The possibility of this cloud of icy objects was suggested by Dutch astronomer Jan Oort in 1950. If the Oort Cloud does exist, its outer objects are the most distant things that feel— weakly—the pull of the Sun's gravity.

KUIPER BELT

Astronomers have now discovered thousands of Kuiper Belt objects (KBOs), but there may be a trillion or more still to be spotted, most of them smaller than 100 km (62 miles) wide. The combined mass of all the KBOs is probably no more than 1 percent of Earth's mass.

SCATTERED DISK

The billions of objects in the Scattered Disk probably used to orbit in the Kuiper Belt, but they were "scattered" by Neptune's gravity, giving them very tilted, elliptical (stretched out) orbits. When closest to the Sun, Scattered Disk objects are in the Kuiper Belt, but they may travel twice as far from the Sun as KBOs: up to 15 billion km (9.3 billion miles).

OORT CLOUD

The Oort Cloud may stretch from 300 billion to 30 trillion km (186 billion to 18.6 trillion miles) from the Sun. The inner cloud may be ring-shaped, while the trillions of objects in the outer cloud form a sphere as they have been scattered by the pull of other stars. Oort Cloud objects may be made of material from the edge of the disk that surrounded the newborn Sun.

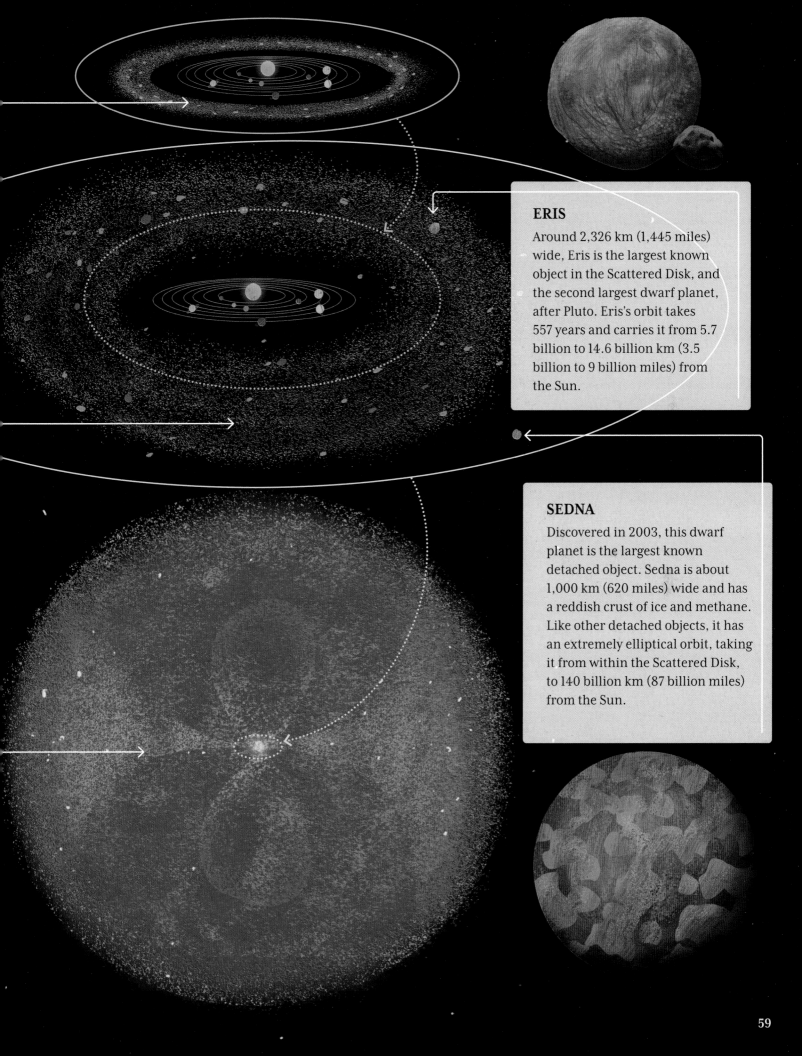

ERIS

Around 2,326 km (1,445 miles) wide, Eris is the largest known object in the Scattered Disk, and the second largest dwarf planet, after Pluto. Eris's orbit takes 557 years and carries it from 5.7 billion to 14.6 billion km (3.5 billion to 9 billion miles) from the Sun.

SEDNA

Discovered in 2003, this dwarf planet is the largest known detached object. Sedna is about 1,000 km (620 miles) wide and has a reddish crust of ice and methane. Like other detached objects, it has an extremely elliptical orbit, taking it from within the Scattered Disk, to 140 billion km (87 billion miles) from the Sun.

Stars and Galaxies

Our star, called the Sun, is one of perhaps 1 septillion stars in the Universe. This number—a 1 followed by 24 zeros—can only be an estimate, as there are far, far too many stars to even begin to count. Just like the Sun, all stars are glowing spheres of gas so hot that it has turned to plasma—its atoms have torn apart, making them electrically charged. Although plasma is uncommon on Earth, in the Universe it is much more common than solids, liquids, or gases.

Most stars are part of a galaxy—a collection of stars, planets, gas, and dust, all held together by the force of gravity. On average, the stars in a galaxy may be around 5 light-years apart, with 1 light-year being the distance that light travels in a year—9.46 trillion km (5.88 trillion miles). Galaxies probably formed from immense, collapsing clouds of gas and dust, where many stars were pressed into life at once. Although stars cannot form in the near emptiness between galaxies, a minority of stars—although there are probably trillions of them altogether—lie between galaxies. Astronomers think these "intergalactic stars" formed inside a galaxy, but were tossed out, perhaps by a collision between galaxies.

The Sun is one of at least 100 billion stars in our galaxy, the Milky Way. In the whole Universe, there are perhaps 2 trillion galaxies of different shapes and sizes. Most galaxies are grouped together with other galaxies to form galaxy clusters, held together by their gravity, even though each galaxy may be more than a million light-years from the next. Galaxy clusters tend to be grouped into superclusters, containing perhaps 200,000 galaxies. There may be up to 10 million superclusters in the Universe.

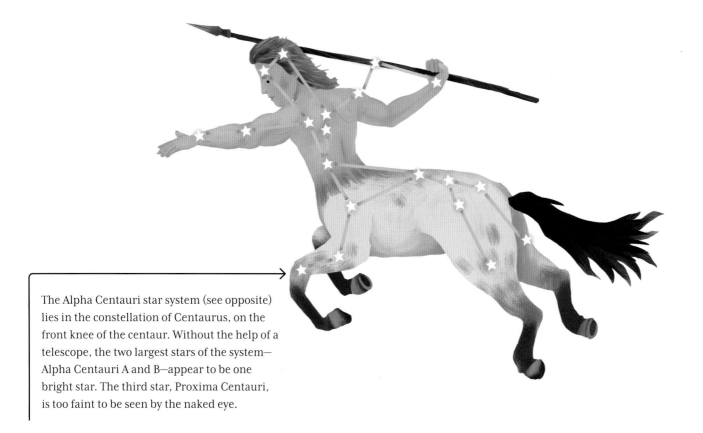

The Alpha Centauri star system (see opposite) lies in the constellation of Centaurus, on the front knee of the centaur. Without the help of a telescope, the two largest stars of the system— Alpha Centauri A and B—appear to be one bright star. The third star, Proxima Centauri, is too faint to be seen by the naked eye.

Around 4.2 light-years away, the nearest star to the Sun is Proxima Centauri, a small reddish star known as a red dwarf. Proxima is part of a triple star system along with the stars Alpha Centauri A and B (top left). A star system is a small number of stars, within a galaxy, that orbit each other. Proxima Centauri is orbited by at least two planets.

Star Chart

When we look at the night sky, groups of stars seem to form the shapes of people, animals, or objects. These patterns are known as constellations. Astronomers agree on 88 official constellations. The stars in a constellation may be trillions of kilometers apart, but they appear close together when viewed from Earth.

PEGASUS

This large constellation takes its name from a winged horse of ancient Greek myths. Hundreds of years before the Greeks named the constellations, Babylonian astronomers saw a four-starred constellation here, called Iku ("field"). Today, those four bright stars are said to form an asterism, known as the Great Square. An asterism is a pattern of stars within one of the official constellations.

EQUULEUS

The name of this small, faint constellation means "little horse" in Latin. It is linked with the young horse Celeris, who in Greek myths was the child of the winged horse Pegasus. The Pegasus constellation lies nearby.

MILKY WAY GALAXY

Our galaxy can be seen as a pale streak of stars and dust as—from our location on Earth—we look at the side of its disk. This paleness earned the galaxy its "milky" name.

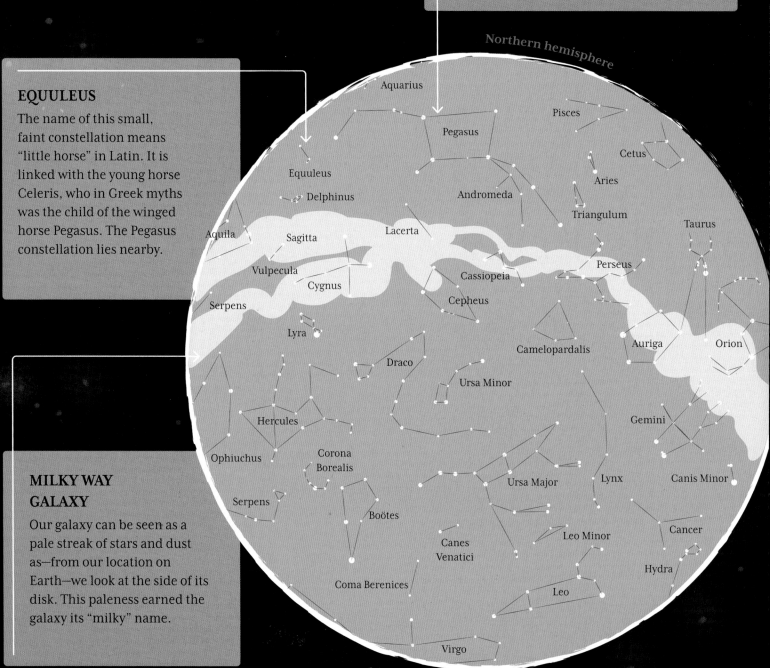

Northern hemisphere

Aquarius • Pisces • Pegasus • Cetus • Aries • Andromeda • Triangulum • Taurus • Equuleus • Delphinus • Aquila • Sagitta • Lacerta • Perseus • Vulpecula • Cassiopeia • Auriga • Orion • Cygnus • Cepheus • Serpens • Lyra • Cameleopardalis • Draco • Ursa Minor • Gemini • Hercules • Canis Minor • Ophiuchus • Corona Borealis • Lynx • Serpens • Ursa Major • Cancer • Boötes • Leo Minor • Hydra • Canes Venatici • Leo • Coma Berenices • Virgo

Around 36 constellations can be seen in the northern hemisphere, from north of Earth's equator, for most of the year. About 52 constellations spend most of the year in the southern skies. Some constellations can be seen from the "other" hemisphere during all or part of the year. For example, the southern constellation Scorpius is visible from southern parts of the northern hemisphere during the summer months.

As our planet rotates over the course of a night, the constellations appear to move from east to west across the sky, just like the Sun appears to do during the day. As Earth orbits the Sun, the constellations also move slowly westward during the year. These changes are due to our changing viewpoint as we look into space.

Southern hemisphere

Cetus · Aquarius · Sculptor · Piscis Austrinus · Capricornus · Fornax · Phoenix · Grus · Microscopium · Aquila · Eridanus · Tucana · Indus · Sagittarius · Scutum · Horologium · Reticulum · Hydrus · Corona Australis · Serpens · Orion · Lepus · Dorado · Pavo · Telescopium · Caelum · Pictor · Octans · Apus · Columba · Mensa Volans · Ara · Scorpius · Canis Major · Carina · Chamaeleon · Triangulum Australe · Ophiuchus · Monoceros · Musca · Circinus · Norma · Puppis · Crux · Vela · Lupus · Pyxis · Centaurus · Libra · Antlia · Hydra · Hydra · Corvus · Virgo · Sextans · Crater

AQUARIUS

Aquarius means "water-carrier" in Latin. More than 3,000 years ago, Babylonian astronomers thought these stars looked like their water god, Ea, as he poured water. The constellation is in part of the sky, known as the Sea due to its constellations linked with water, including Cetus ("whale"), Piscis Austrinus ("southern fish"), and Eridanus ("river").

OPHIUCHUS

The ancient Greeks saw Ophiuchus ("serpent-bearer") as a man wrestling a snake. His snake was seen in the nearby constellation Serpens ("serpent"). In fact, Ophiuchus divides Serpens in two—Caput ("head") and Cauda ("tail"). Both constellations are on the night sky's equator, crossing between the northern and southern hemispheres.

Northern Constellations

Most northern constellations are based on patterns seen by Greek astronomers over 2,000 years ago. Many are named after characters and creatures from Greek myths. Yet the Greeks based their constellations on those mapped by the Babylonians hundreds of years earlier.

ORION

Orion was a hunter who, according to one Greek myth, was killed by a scorpion. Seen in the southern constellation Scorpius, crossing the night sky's equator, Orion can be identified by the three stars that form his belt.

CASSIOPEIA

Cassiopeia is one of the most easily spotted northern constellations, due to its five bright stars forming a W shape. In Greek myths, Cassiopeia was a queen who boasted of her own beauty.

TAURUS

Taurus ("bull") is one of the 12 zodiac constellations. Watched from Earth, the Sun seems to pass in front of these constellations over the year. Zodiac means "path of little animals" in ancient Greek, as many of these constellations, including Leo and Scorpius, are represented by animals.

GEMINI

Seen clearly during winter nights, Gemini ("twins") is linked with twin brothers of Greek myth named Pollux and Castor. The constellation's brightest stars are Pollux, which forms the head of the left brother, and Castor, which forms the head of his brother.

LEO

This bright constellation takes its name from the Latin for "lion." The ancient Greeks associated these stars with the lion killed by Hercules, a great hero of their myths.

URSA MAJOR AND URSA MINOR

Tracing a line from the two brightest stars of Ursa Major ("bigger bear") takes us to Polaris, the North Pole Star, which is in Ursa Minor ("smaller bear"). Polaris always lies over the North Pole, making it useful for finding the direction of north.

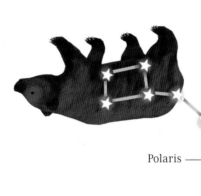

Polaris

Polaris Facts

OBJECT	Yellow supergiant star
MASS	5.4 Suns
SIZE	52 million km (32 million miles) across
TEMPERATURE	5,740 °C (10,364 °F) at the photosphere
AGE	70 million years
LOCATION	433 light-years from Earth

Southern Constellations

Peoples of the southern hemisphere named these stars long ago, but today's official international names were given by European astronomers. The constellations visible from Europe were named by the ancient Greeks, while the rest were named after the 16th century, when Europeans began exploring south of the equator.

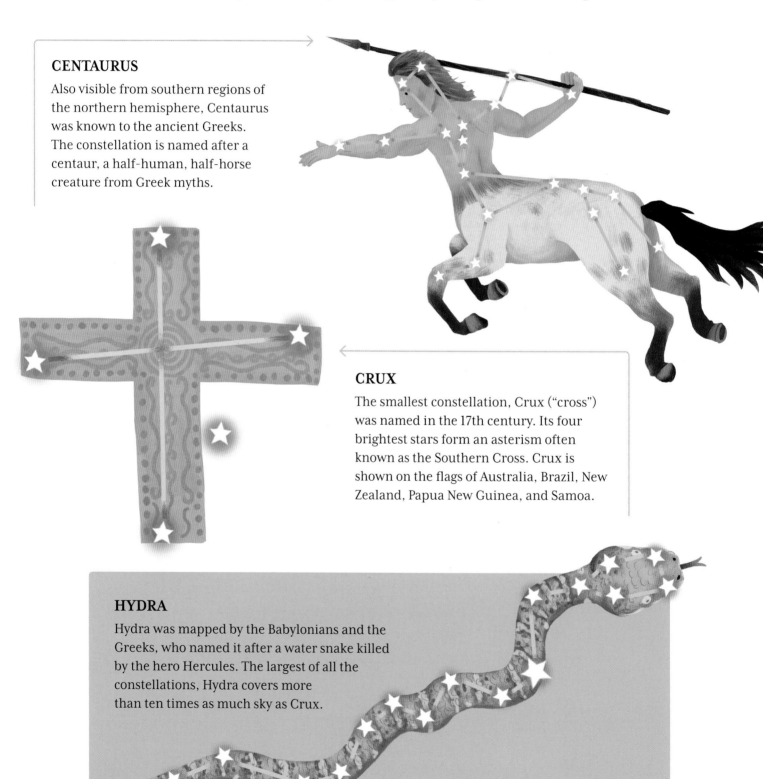

CENTAURUS

Also visible from southern regions of the northern hemisphere, Centaurus was known to the ancient Greeks. The constellation is named after a centaur, a half-human, half-horse creature from Greek myths.

CRUX

The smallest constellation, Crux ("cross") was named in the 17th century. Its four brightest stars form an asterism often known as the Southern Cross. Crux is shown on the flags of Australia, Brazil, New Zealand, Papua New Guinea, and Samoa.

HYDRA

Hydra was mapped by the Babylonians and the Greeks, who named it after a water snake killed by the hero Hercules. The largest of all the constellations, Hydra covers more than ten times as much sky as Crux.

CANIS MAJOR

Along with Canis Minor ("smaller dog"), Canis Major ("bigger dog") seems to follow the hunter Orion across the sky. The brightest star in the sky, Sirius, lies on the dog's chest. Its brightness is due to being only 81 trillion km (50 trillion miles) from Earth.

SCORPIUS

Named after a scorpion from Greek mythology, Scorpius was known to the Babylonians as Mul Gir-Tab ("creature with a burning sting"). Its brightest star, Antares, is on the scorpion's head.

OCTANS

In 1752, this constellation was named after the octant, a measuring instrument that helped sailors to navigate. The faint South Pole Star, also known as Sigma Octantis, lies in the constellation.

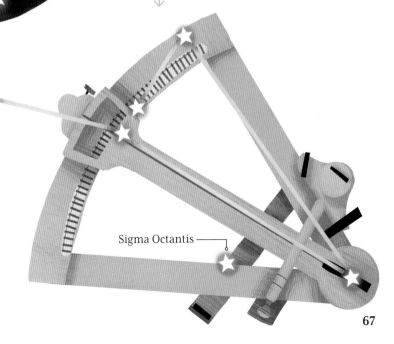

Sigma Octantis

Sigma Octantis Facts

OBJECT	Yellow giant star
MASS	1.6 Suns
SIZE	6.1 million km (3.8 million miles) across
TEMPERATURE	7,140 °C (12,884 °F) at the photosphere
AGE	912 million years
LOCATION	294 light-years from Earth

Star Types

Astronomers divide stars into types based on their size, temperature, and brightness. Usually, the heavier a star is, the hotter and brighter it is. Astronomers can identify a star's type by examining the light that it gives off.

STAR SIZES

From largest to smallest, the different sizes of stars have names, including hypergiant, supergiant, giant, and dwarf. The Sun is a dwarf, as are the majority of stars in the Universe. While the Sun is 1,390,000 km (864,000 miles) across, one of the largest known stars, the hypergiant UY Scuti, is 2,376,000,000 km (1,476,000,000 miles) wide. If it were placed in the middle of our Solar System, it would stretch past Jupiter.

Annie Jump Cannon used a magnifying glass to examine glass photographic plates. Since photography was then only in black and white, the plates did not actually show the different shades of starlight, but each star spectrum was broken up by black lines that made it possible to figure the shades out.

RAINBOW STARS

The light given off by stars is made up of all the shades of the rainbow—red, orange, yellow, green, blue, and violet—known as the spectrum (see pages 88–89). Yet stars with different temperatures give off different amounts of these shades. The hottest stars give off more light in the blue part of the spectrum. Cooler stars give off more yellow light, while even cooler stars are reddish. In fact, the human eye may not see these differences in shade clearly. For example, the Sun is classified as a yellow star, but our eyes see its light as white.

ANNIE'S STARS

Annie Jump Cannon was an astronomer who, in 1901, came up with a system for classifying stars—or placing them into different types. She worked at the Harvard College Observatory, in the United States, where the light from stars was split into its separate shades using a glass prism—like raindrops bend and split sunlight, creating a rainbow. The prism was placed in front of a telescope's eyepiece, then the resulting pattern was captured on a photographic plate.

Annie examined the plates to classify each star by its shade. She rearranged the existing star classification—in which stars were identified alphabetically—and suggested what is known as the Harvard system of star classification. The system uses the letters O, B, A, F, G, K, and M—with O the hottest and bluest, and M the coolest. Dying stars such as white dwarfs (see page 71) were not included in the classification. Today, Roman numerals have been added to the system to show brightness, also called luminosity. From brightest to darkest, these rankings are 0, I, II, III, IV, V, VI, and VII. For being a yellow star, the Sun is classified as G, while for being medium-bright it gets a V.

An O-type star has a surface temperature of over 29,700 °C (53,500 °F), while an M is less than 3,400 °C (6,150 °F).

O   B   A F G K M

Star Birth and Death

Stars are born in clouds of gas and dust. All stars eventually die. Over the course of one year in our Milky Way Galaxy, around seven stars are born, while at least one star dies. Some stars have short lives and violent deaths, while others live long and die quietly.

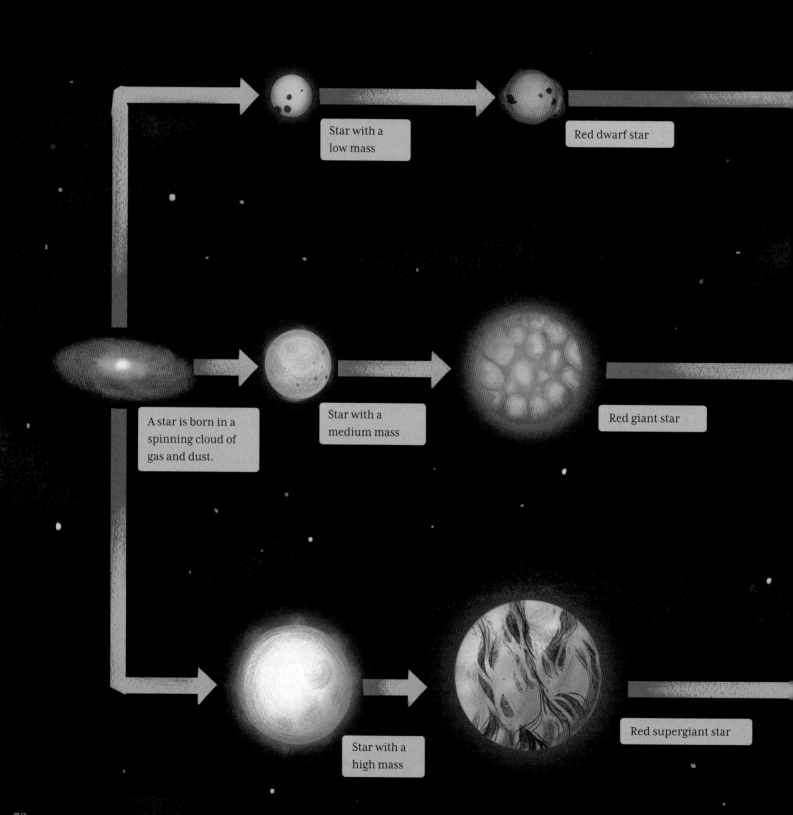

Star with a low mass

Red dwarf star

A star is born in a spinning cloud of gas and dust.

Star with a medium mass

Red giant star

Star with a high mass

Red supergiant star

A star is born when a cloud of gas and dust collapses. At the core of the cloud, a tightly squeezed sphere of material grows. Here, atoms of hydrogen start to crash into each other, joining to become helium atoms. This releases energy, making the sphere glow as a newborn star. A star lives until it runs out of hydrogen, which is its fuel. Then the star begins to change—and eventually to die.

Although stars with a greater mass (or weight) contain more hydrogen, their greater mass also makes their gravity stronger—making hydrogen atoms crash together more quickly in their core. This means that massive stars use up their hydrogen fuel in perhaps a few million years. Massive stars die in an explosion known as a supernova. Smaller stars use their fuel more slowly, then die more peacefully. The smallest stars may live for trillions of years.

White dwarf

LOW-MASS STAR DEATH

If a star has less than half the mass of the Sun, it dies quietly. When it runs out of hydrogen, it slowly shrinks, cools, and fades, becoming a white dwarf. Around the size of Earth, a white dwarf is the "dead" remains of a star. Over billions of years, a white dwarf will probably grow so cool that it becomes a black dwarf. However, the Universe is not yet old enough for any black dwarfs to exist.

MEDIUM-MASS STAR DEATH

Planetary nebula

White dwarf

A Sun-sized star takes around 10 billion years to run out of hydrogen. Then it expands, becoming a red giant star. In the star's core, helium atoms crash together to become carbon and oxygen atoms. The intense heat from this process sends out a vast cloud of gas and dust, called a planetary nebula. After around 10,000 years, the cloud drifts away, leaving behind only a white dwarf, which may eventually fade into a black dwarf.

Neutron star

HIGH-MASS STAR DEATH

If a star is over 8 times more massive than the Sun, it expands into a red supergiant star when it runs out of hydrogen. Then, after it goes through its helium and other fuels, its core collapses, creating a huge explosion known as a supernova. Stars up to 25 times the Sun's mass collapse into a neutron star, while bigger stars collapse into a black hole (see page 72). Only around 10 km (6 miles) wide, a neutron star still has a mass greater than the Sun. Some spin super-fast and give out beams

Supernova

Black hole

Black Holes

A black hole is an area of space with very intense gravity. Anything that comes too close to a black hole cannot escape its pull. Black holes can form when massive stars die, but a mysterious black hole also lies at the heart of most galaxies.

PULLING SPACE AND TIME

Gravity is the force that pulls all objects toward each other. The bigger an object's mass, the stronger its gravity. If a huge mass is squeezed into a really small space—as happens when a massive star collapses—its gravity can stretch space itself, making a black hole. A black hole gains its name from the fact that even light cannot escape its pull, making it look black.

The region at the heart of a black hole is called a singularity. Anything that falls into the singularity—such as stars and dust—is crushed infinitely small, and its mass is added to the mass of the black hole. Strangely, the gravity of a singularity stretches time itself, so a clock close to a black hole would tick more slowly than a clock farther away.

FALLING INSIDE

The singularity is surrounded by a boundary known as the event horizon. Inside this boundary, the black hole looks black. If anything crosses the event horizon, it cannot escape because it would need to travel faster than the speed of light, which nothing can do. For an ordinary-sized black hole, the event horizon may be just 30 km (18.6 miles) from one side to the other.

The term "event horizon" comes from the fact that, if an event took place within the boundary (or horizon), information from that event could not reach anyone outside the boundary, making it impossible to know if the event took place.

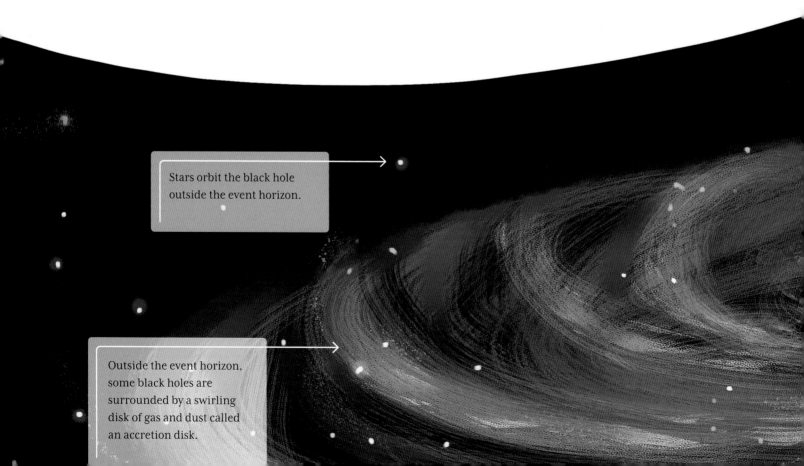

Stars orbit the black hole outside the event horizon.

Outside the event horizon, some black holes are surrounded by a swirling disk of gas and dust called an accretion disk.

GALAXY HEARTS

The black holes at the heart of most galaxies are called supermassive black holes because they are much bigger than ordinary black holes. They may have a mass billions of times that of the Sun. Astronomers are not sure how these black holes formed. Perhaps an ordinary-sized black hole grew larger as it sucked in material or joined with another black hole, then its gravity collected stars and dust around it, forming a galaxy. It is also possible that the supermassive black hole formed at the same time as the galaxy, as a cloud of gas and dust collapsed, forming multiple stars around a central black hole.

Sagittarius A* Facts

OBJECT	Supermassive black hole
MASS	4 million Suns
SIZE	24 million km (15 million miles) across the event horizon
TEMPERATURE	10 million °C (18 million °F) in the accretion disk
AGE	Possibly 13.6 billion years
LOCATION	26,000 light-years from Earth

The Sagittarius A* supermassive black hole lies at the middle of the Milky Way Galaxy, but it rarely pulls in gas or dust.

Exoplanets

The Sun is not the only star with planets in orbit around it. In fact, astronomers believe that most stars host one or more planets, giving them what is called a planetary system. Planets that orbit a star other than the Sun are known as exoplanets.

UNIVERSE OF PLANETS

Since the first exoplanet was spotted in 1992, astronomers have discovered more than 5,000 of them through their telescopes. They believe many trillions more may exist. Just like there are different types of planets in our Solar System, there are different types of exoplanets. There are rock and metal Earth-like planets, gas giants like Jupiter, and ice giants like Neptune. In addition, there are "hot Jupiters," which are gas giants that orbit very close to their star, as well as "super-Earths," which are similar to Earth, but much larger.

LOOKING FOR LIFE

Astronomers are excited by exoplanets because if one of the eight planets in our planetary system is home to life, it is possible an exoplanet is, too. Exoplanets are too far away to look for signs of life through a telescope. It would take more than 6,000 years for a space probe to reach the closest exoplanets, which orbit the nearest star, Proxima Centauri (see page 61). Instead, astronomers study the likely conditions on exoplanets to see if they could be habitable (or suitable for life).

The first factor to consider is the materials of the exoplanet. Since gas giants and ice giants have no solid surface, they probably cannot be home to life. Another factor is an exoplanet's distance from its star. Water is

needed by all known living things. If a planet is too close to its star, water would boil away. If it is too far away, all water would freeze. Between these extremes is a habitable zone. Astronomers also look at the nature of each star. If, for example, a star has bursts of energy, it could make its planets uninhabitable. Considering all these factors, astronomers estimate there are 11 billion habitable exoplanets in the Milky Way Galaxy alone.

TOI-700 d Facts

OBJECT	Exoplanet
MASS	Around 1.7 Earths
SIZE	Around 15,160 km (9,420 miles) across
MOONS	None known
ROTATION	Possibly 37 days
ORBIT	37 days
TEMPERATURE	Possibly 22 °C (72 °F) on the surface
LOCATION	An average 24.4 million km (15.2 million miles) from TOI-700

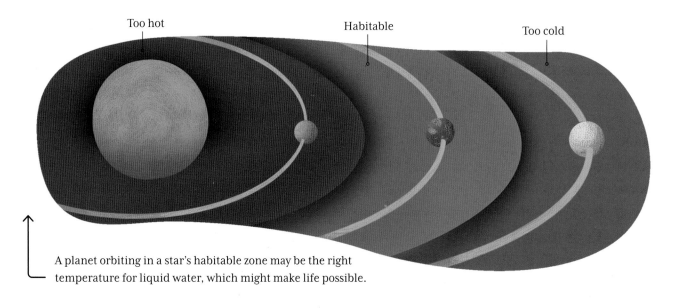

Too hot · Habitable · Too cold

A planet orbiting in a star's habitable zone may be the right temperature for liquid water, which might make life possible.

Around 101 light-years from Earth, the red dwarf star TOI-700 is orbited by four exoplanets. In order of distance from the star, they are TOI-700 b, c, e, and d. TOI-700 d is an Earth-like planet in the habitable zone. This illustration imagines it has oceans, although we cannot know that for sure.

Galaxies

The smallest galaxies, known as dwarf galaxies, have a few hundred stars.
The largest, called supergiant galaxies, contain 100 trillion stars, all held
together by gravity and all spinning around the galaxy's central point.
Galaxies have three main shapes—spirals, ellipticals, and irregular.

SPIRAL GALAXIES

Around two-thirds of galaxies have a spiral shape.
These galaxies are spinning disks with curving arms of
thicker stars, gas, and dust stretching from their core.
At the core is a bulge of stars that may be roughly circular
(pictured) or stretched into a bar (see page 78).

ELLIPTICAL GALAXIES

These galaxies are the shape of a flattened ball.
Although some elliptical galaxies are small,
the Universe's largest galaxies are elliptical.
While spiral galaxies contain many young
stars, ellipticals have many old stars.
Ellipticals probably formed over time, as
smaller spiral galaxies joined together.

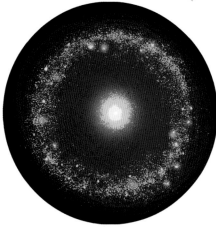

IRREGULAR GALAXIES

A quarter of galaxies are neither
spiral nor elliptical. These irregular
galaxies may look "messy" (left) or
have a strange shape, such as a
ring (right). Irregular galaxies are
usually dwarfs and may have been
deformed by the gravity of a larger
galaxy. A ring shape could have been
made when a small galaxy crashed
through the middle of a larger one.

VERA RUBIN

Vera Rubin was an American astronomer who studied galaxies and concluded in 1978, that there must be more matter in them than what could be seen. This invisible matter is called dark matter. Like ordinary matter—from dogs to dust and stars—dark matter has gravity. By studying the speed of stars spinning around the core of their galaxy, Rubin figured out there must be lots of dark matter in a galaxy, creating lots of extra gravity.

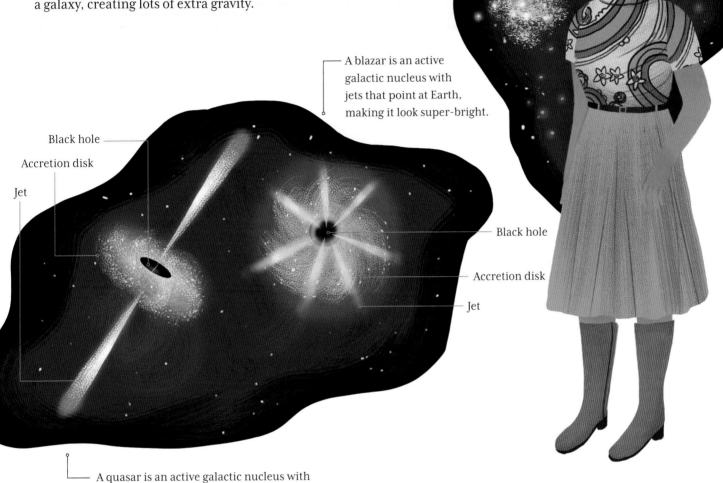

A blazar is an active galactic nucleus with jets that point at Earth, making it look super-bright.

Black hole

Accretion disk

Jet

Black hole

Accretion disk

Jet

A quasar is an active galactic nucleus with jets that point away from us.

ACTIVE GALACTIC NUCLEI

There are old galaxies and young galaxies. Some young galaxies have a very bright central area called an active galactic nucleus. Most galaxies have a supermassive black hole at their heart, but these younger galaxies have black holes that pull in lots of material. As this material circles the black hole, it gets so hot it emits jets of powerful energy. The black holes at the hearts of old galaxies are much quieter because they have run out of nearby material to suck inside.

3C 273 Facts

OBJECT	Blazar at the middle of a giant elliptical galaxy
MASS	886 million Suns
JETS	200,000 light-years long
BRIGHTNESS	4 trillion times brighter than the Sun
TEMPERATURE	10 trillion °C (18 trillion °F)
LOCATION	2.4 billion light-years from Earth

The Milky Way

The Milky Way is a spiral galaxy with a central bar of stars. Our galaxy is around 100,000 light-years across, but only about 2,000 light-years thick. It has at least 100 billion stars, perhaps as many as 400 billion. The galaxy takes around 230 million years to rotate once about its central point.

From our position in the Milky Way's disk, it is difficult to know the exact shape of the galaxy's curving arms. Yet astronomers have pieced together evidence by observing other galaxies and measuring the movements of the stars in our own. By looking at the night sky, we can tell that we do not live in an elliptical galaxy. If we did, we would see the stars and dust of our galaxy spread across the sky, rather than in a narrow band.

The Milky Way probably started to form not long after the Universe's very first stars, around 13.7 billion years ago. The oldest stars in the Milky Way date from this time, while its youngest stars probably formed within the last year. Over the billions of years since our galaxy's birth, it has grown by merging with other galaxies. Today, it continues to grow by pulling in material from the 59 smaller galaxies in orbit around it, known as satellite galaxies. The biggest of these satellites is the Large Magellanic Cloud, around 32,200 light-years across and 160,000 light-years away.

THE SOLAR SYSTEM

The Sun is around 28,000 light-years from the middle of the Milky Way, in the Orion-Cygnus arm. This minor arm lies inside the major Perseus arm and may be a branch of it.

PERSEUS ARM

The Perseus arm begins from the end of the central bar that is farthest from our Solar System. It is named after the Perseus constellation of stars as it can be seen in this direction when viewed from Earth.

NORMA ARM

This minor arm of the Milky Way stretches from its central bar. It is named for the southern constellation of Norma, through which it seems to pass.

GLOBULAR CLUSTER

A globular cluster is a roughly ball-shaped group of stars, held together by gravity. These clusters are found within the Milky Way's disk and beyond it, in the more loosely scattered stars of the galactic halo.

CENTRAL BAR

The galaxy's bar cuts across its central region, with a bulge of old yellow stars at its middle. It is here that the supermassive black hole Sagittarius A* is found.

SCUTUM-CENTAURUS ARM

This major arm begins from the nearest end of the Milky Way's central bar. Like the galaxy's other arms, it is thick with stars, gas, and dust. New stars form among its dense clouds.

The Local Group and Beyond

The Milky Way is one of at least 80 galaxies in a galaxy cluster called the Local Group. The Local Group is one of over 100 clusters in the Virgo Supercluster. Our supercluster is part of the Pisces–Cetus Supercluster Complex, a vast wall of superclusters known as a galaxy filament.

If the distance from the Milky Way to the next large galaxy seems vast, the distance to the next galaxy cluster or the next supercluster—around 300 million light-years—becomes dizzying. In fact, there are some distances so vast that we can never even know them. We cannot know the size of the whole Universe. We do not know if it continues forever or not. When astronomers discuss the size of the Universe, they talk about the "observable Universe." This is the ball-shaped portion of it that can be seen from Earth, because its light (which our eyes and telescopes detect) has had time to reach us since the Big Bang.

Since it is 13.8 billion years since the Big Bang, we might think that the observable Universe would extend for only 13.8 billion light-years in every direction. However, the objects that gave off light 13.8 billion years ago have since moved farther away from us due to the growth of the Universe—and they are now 46.5 billion light-years away. This means that the distance across the observable Universe—with Earth at its middle—is twice that—93 billion light-years.

LOCAL GROUP

Around 10 million light-years across, the Local Group contains two collections of galaxies—the Milky Way and its satellite galaxies, and the Andromeda Galaxy and its satellites. The mass of the whole cluster is around 2 trillion Suns.

VIRGO SUPERCLUSTER

The Local Group is about 65 million light-years from the middle of the Virgo Supercluster. Some astronomers think this supercluster may be part of an even larger supercluster, known as Laniakea.

THE OBSERVABLE UNIVERSE

Superclusters are grouped together into yet larger structures called filaments, with nearly empty space—known as voids—between them. This gives the observable Universe an almost sponge-like appearance.

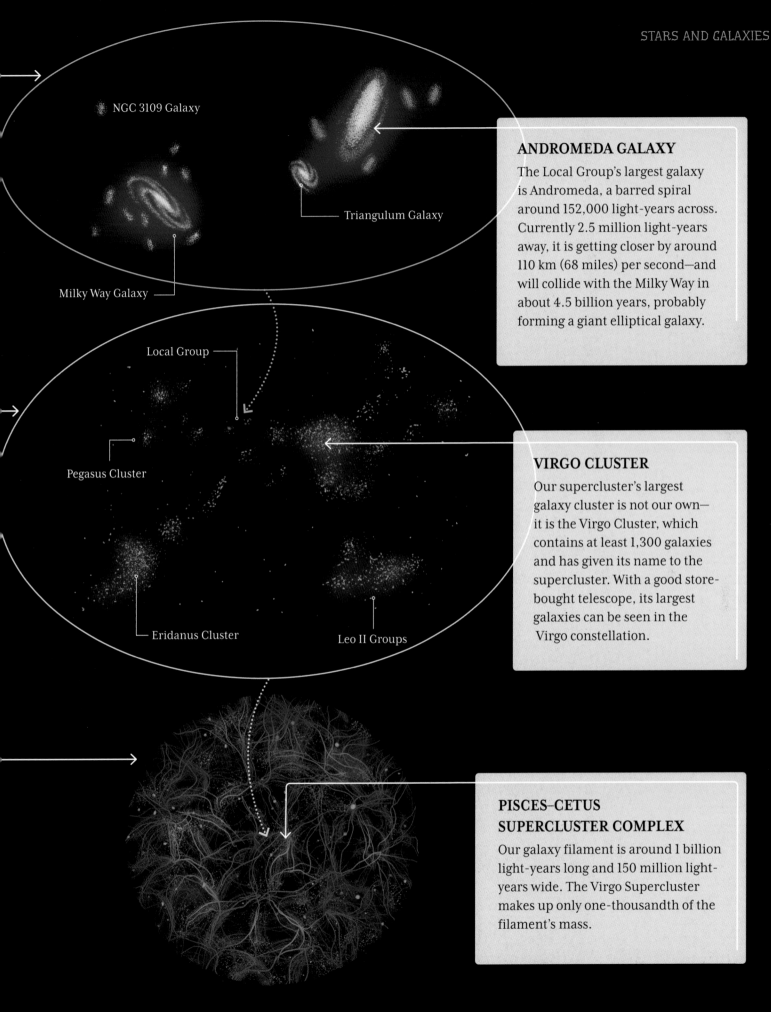

NGC 3109 Galaxy

Triangulum Galaxy

Milky Way Galaxy

ANDROMEDA GALAXY

The Local Group's largest galaxy is Andromeda, a barred spiral around 152,000 light-years across. Currently 2.5 million light-years away, it is getting closer by around 110 km (68 miles) per second—and will collide with the Milky Way in about 4.5 billion years, probably forming a giant elliptical galaxy.

Local Group

Pegasus Cluster

Eridanus Cluster

Leo II Groups

VIRGO CLUSTER

Our supercluster's largest galaxy cluster is not our own—it is the Virgo Cluster, which contains at least 1,300 galaxies and has given its name to the supercluster. With a good store-bought telescope, its largest galaxies can be seen in the Virgo constellation.

PISCES–CETUS SUPERCLUSTER COMPLEX

Our galaxy filament is around 1 billion light-years long and 150 million light-years wide. The Virgo Supercluster makes up only one-thousandth of the filament's mass.

Astronomy

Astronomy is the study of the Universe and everything it holds, from stars to comets, planets to black holes. The word "astronomy" comes from the ancient Greek words for "law of the stars." Yet the first astronomers lived long before the ancient Greeks began writing about the stars around 2,500 years ago. The very earliest attempts to record the positions of the stars may have been over 10,000 years ago, when maps of constellations were painted on the walls of caves.

From the beginning, there have been two branches of astronomy, although early astronomers would not have given their activities these names. The first branch is observational astronomy, which is based on observing (or watching) space objects. Before the invention of the telescope in around 1608, observational astronomy was limited to the objects that could be seen with the naked eye—the Moon, the Sun and other visible stars, the five planets nearest Earth, and some more distant, bright events such as supernovas. From the 19th century, one new invention after another—from the camera in 1826 to the rocket in 1944—led to new discoveries.

The second branch is theoretical astronomy, which is based on developing ideas—called theories—to explain space objects, then trying to prove those theories through observation. Mathematics has always been at the heart of theoretical astronomy, even when the 2nd-century Roman astronomer Ptolemy used calculations to try to prove—incorrectly—that the Sun moves around Earth. Later theoretical astronomers from Isaac Newton to Albert Einstein and Stephen Hawking developed theories that explain the nature of the Universe itself, from the pull of gravity to the death of stars.

Between 1905 and 1915, the German-born scientist Albert Einstein developed his theory of "relativity," which describes how gravity bends space and time. His theory predicted the existence of black holes long before the first photo of one was taken in 2019.

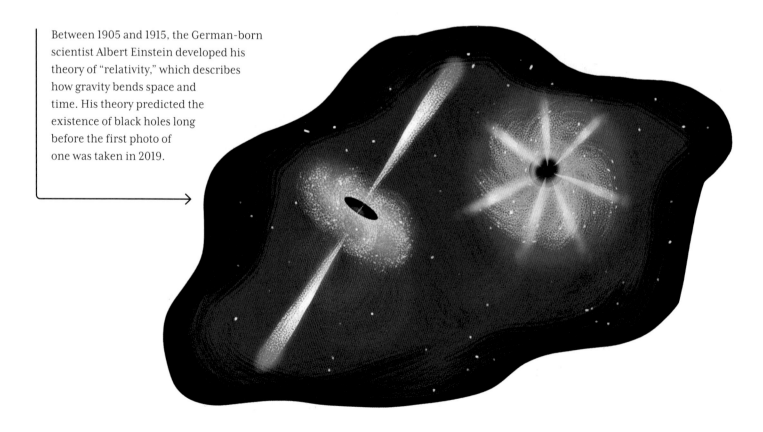

In 10th-century Iran, the observational astronomer Abd al-Rahman al-Sufi made maps of 48 star constellations. He was the first person to record a sighting of a galaxy other than the Milky Way, when he described the Andromeda Galaxy as a "small cloud."

83

Early Ideas

Early astronomers were priests who saw the Sun, Moon, planets, and stars as gods. Yet when these astronomers watched space objects move, they noticed patterns. Slowly, over many centuries, astronomy separated from religion, became attached to mathematics—and became a science.

GODS AND PRIESTS

From the Mayan priest-astronomers of Central America, to the Babylonians of the Middle East, early astronomers used their observations of space objects to create calendars. These charted the seasons so that festivals, seed-sowing, and harvesting took place at the right times.

Even early priest-astronomers used mathematics to track movements and calculate when special events would take place. By around 800 BCE, the Babylonians could predict eclipses of the Sun and Moon many years ahead. Since eclipses of the Moon were believed to bring the gods' anger down on Babylonian kings, a replacement king was put in place for the predicted day. The replacement was put to death, while the real king went unharmed.

DEVELOPING THEORIES

A few centuries after the Babylonians, the ancient Greeks felt that astronomy had little to do with gods and everything to do with mathematics. They started to look for practical reasons for the movements of space objects, and to come up with theories to explain the known Universe. As early as the 3rd century BCE, Aristarchus of Samos suggested the—correct—theory that Earth and the other planets rotated around the Sun.

Yet it was a different theory of the Solar System that became popular for hundreds of years. Ptolemy was an astronomer from a Greek family who lived in Roman-ruled Egypt during the 2nd century CE. He wrote that the Sun and planets revolved around Earth. This idea—which matched humankind's feeling of being central to creation—was not fully disproved until the Scientific Revolution.

The Maya calendar had two cycles, which matched up every 52 years. The Haab followed Earth's orbit around the Sun and lasted 365 days, divided into 19 months (outer brown circle). The Tzolkin, which was used for timing festivals, lasted 260 days and was divided into 13 sets (inner white circle) of 20 days (green circle).

SCIENTIFIC REVOLUTION

The Scientific Revolution was a period in the 16th and 17th centuries when ideas about the Universe were completely changed by breakthroughs in astronomy, mathematics, and science. During this time, modern science—based on the scientific method—took shape. The scientific method is the process of observing, asking questions, and finding answers through experiments, calculations, and further observations.

In 1543, the Scientific Revolution began when the Polish astronomer Nicolaus Copernicus published mathematical calculations showing that Earth revolves around the Sun. His work was later backed up by Italian astronomer Galileo Galilei, using observations he made with his telescope. The idea was so shocking that, in 1633, Galileo was sentenced to imprisonment in his own home. Yet, before the end of the 17th century, the theory was becoming widely accepted.

In around 906 CE, the Maya built an observatory in their city Chichén Itzá, in modern Mexico. The tall building let them watch the sky above the surrounding buildings and forest.

Windows aligned with the direction of sunset on the equinoxes (when the Sun is directly above the equator) and with Venus's northernmost position in the sky. Venus was important to the Maya, who timed their battles for its appearance in the morning sky.

Astronomers

In 1666, the great British astronomer Isaac Newton figured out some of the basic rules that govern the Universe—the laws of gravity. Since then, astronomers have taken more and more steps toward understanding the strange, exciting Universe.

ISAAC NEWTON

Newton figured out that a force, which he called gravity, attracts every particle in the Universe to every other particle. This breakthrough explained why an apple falls to the ground and the planets orbit the Sun—and was the foundation of modern astronomy.

SUBRAHMANYAN CHANDRASEKHAR

In the 1930s, Indian-born Chandrasekhar figured out why and how stars die when they run out of hydrogen fuel (see page 70). He determined the "Chandrasekhar limit," above which a star will explode as a supernova.

CAROLINE HERSCHEL

This German-British astronomer was paid a salary for her work, making her the first female professional astronomer. Between 1786 and 1797, she discovered eight comets using her telescope.

Stephen Hawking Facts

1942	He is born in Oxford, England.
1963	He is diagnosed with motor neurone disease, which gradually paralyses him.
1970	With mathematician Roger Penrose, he proves the Big Bang started from an infinitely small point, called a singularity.
1974	He predicts that black holes must give off energy, called Hawking radiation, as they shrink.
1983	With physicist James Hartle, he suggests the Big Bang created space, swiftly followed by time.
2018	He dies in Cambridge, England.

STEPHEN HAWKING

Hawking combined the laws of gravity with the laws of "quantum mechanics," which govern the nature of atoms. This allowed him to create equations that describe the whole history of the Universe.

JOCELYN BELL BURNELL

In 1967, when she was 24 years old, this Northern Irish astronomer discovered the first pulsar. This is a spinning neutron star (see page 71) that blasts out energy from its poles.

ANDREA GHEZ

In 2003, Ghez proved that a supermassive black hole, called Sagittarius A*, lies at the Milky Way's heart. Although the black hole cannot be seen, Ghez has watched the stars orbiting it to figure out its mass and size.

87

Electromagnetic Radiation

Astronomers can observe most space objects because they emit (give off) electromagnetic radiation. This is energy that travels through space at the speed of light. The light we can see is one form of electromagnetic radiation, but different types of objects emit other forms.

INFRARED

Everything that has heat emits infrared. Much infrared is absorbed by Earth's atmosphere, and it is difficult to detect accurately because telescopes themselves emit infrared. However, infrared space telescopes observe objects—such as planets—that are too distant and cool to be detected in visible light.

VISIBLE LIGHT

Most stars give off the majority of their electromagnetic energy as visible light. This is the only form of electromagnetic radiation that can be seen by human eyes.

MICROWAVES

Earth's atmosphere blocks most microwaves, so they are detected by telescopes orbiting in space, known as space telescopes. Microwave maps of the sky (pictured below) show that the whole sky is a source of microwaves, the faint leftovers of the radiation created by the Big Bang.

RADIO WAVES

Radio waves pass easily through the atmosphere, so radio telescopes are often located on the ground. This form of radiation is emitted by many space objects, but strong sources include clouds of gas and dust.

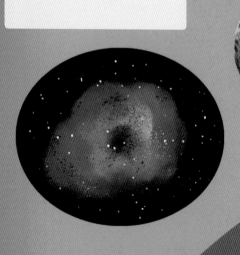

Electromagnetic radiation is a stream of particles called photons, each of them moving in a wave-like pattern. Photons are packets of energy. This energy is called electromagnetic energy because it was made by the movement of electrically charged particles, such as electrons and protons (see page 6).

The different forms of electromagnetic radiation are together known as the electromagnetic spectrum. Different forms are made up of photons carrying different amounts of energy, which gives their waves different wavelengths—the distance between the peaks of the waves. At one end of the electromagnetic spectrum are radio waves, made up of low-energy photons with long wavelengths. At the other end are gamma rays, with high-energy photons that have short wavelengths.

We see these wavelengths as the shades of the rainbow, known as the spectrum. Each shade has a different wavelength, with red being the longest and violet the shortest. When all the wavelengths are seen together, they make white light.

ULTRAVIOLET

Earth's atmosphere absorbs most ultraviolet, so this form of radiation must be detected by space telescopes. Energetic young stars are strong sources of ultraviolet.

X-RAYS

This high-energy radiation is emitted particularly by super-hot gas from events such as supernovas. X-rays are blocked by Earth's atmosphere and are difficult to record by space telescopes because they pass through many materials.

GAMMA RAYS

Gamma rays are emitted by violent objects such as pulsars and blazars. The technology to detect this radiation was not built until 1961, because gamma rays are very difficult to focus on so they can be detected accurately.

Optical Telescopes

Optical telescopes can gather and focus more visible light than the human eye. This means they create brighter and magnified (or larger) images of distant objects. Due to the time light takes to travel from a space object to a telescope, an optical telescope allows us to look back in time.

FOCUSING LIGHT

Some optical telescopes used by astronomers are located on Earth, in observatories on mountaintops where their view is not spoiled by clouds, pollution, or city lights. Other optical telescopes, such as the Hubble Space Telescope, orbit above Earth's atmosphere to get an even clearer view.

Powerful optical telescopes are usually reflecting telescopes. They have a curved primary mirror, which gathers light. The wider the primary mirror, the more light it can collect to make dim objects look brighter. The primary mirror reflects light onto a flat secondary mirror, which reflects and focusses the light into an eyepiece. Here, it passes through a lens that magnifies the image.

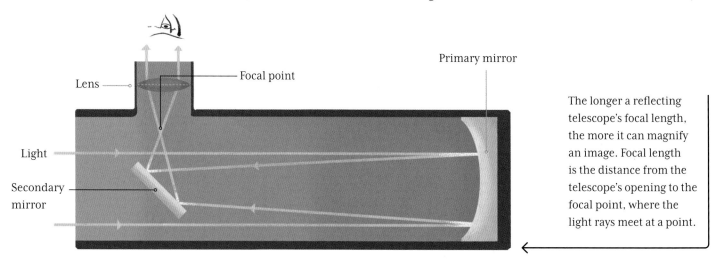

Lens — Focal point

Primary mirror

Light

Secondary mirror

The longer a reflecting telescope's focal length, the more it can magnify an image. Focal length is the distance from the telescope's opening to the focal point, where the light rays meet at a point.

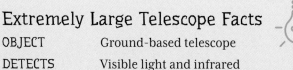

Extremely Large Telescope Facts

OBJECT	Ground-based telescope
DETECTS	Visible light and infrared
MIRRORS	5 mirrors with a 39.3-m (129-ft) wide primary and 4-m (13-ft) wide secondary
MASS	200,000 kg (440,000 lb) primary mirror
SIZE	74 x 86 m (243 x 282 ft) dome
LAUNCH	2028
LOCATION	3,046 m (9,993 ft) above sea level in Antofagasta, Chile

SEEING THE PAST

The most powerful optical telescopes can detect the light from stars billions of light-years away. For example, in 2022, the Hubble Space Telescope spotted the star Earendel, which is currently 28 billion light-years away. Yet the light from that star had taken only 13 billion years to reach the telescope.

When that light was emitted by the star, not long after the Big Bang, Earendel was just 4 billion light-years from the young Milky Way. The expansion of the Universe has since carried the star much farther away. In fact, Earendel is probably now dead, but Hubble is seeing the star as it was when it first formed. The further away a telescope can look, the further back in time we can see.

When completed, the Extremely Large Telescope (ELT) will be the world's largest optical telescope. It has five mirrors, creating a focal length of 743 m (2,438 ft) by bouncing light between them. The telescope is on a mountain in Chile's Atacama Desert, where the dry air creates few clouds.

Radio Telescopes

A radio telescope usually has a curved "dish" that collects radio waves from space objects such as the Sun, quasars, and pulsars. Since radio waves from such distances are weak, a very large dish is needed to gather them. Many radio telescopes are in groups, so they can work together.

COLLECTING WAVES

Radio telescopes, also called antennas, are located far from towns and cities, so that they are not disturbed by the radio waves emitted from radio stations, phones, and other electronic equipment. The most powerful radio telescopes have a dish that is curved in a shape, called a parabola. The dish can usually be tilted to face different areas of the sky.

The parabola shape reflects incoming radio waves onto a single point above it, called the focus. Positioned at the focus is a "subreflector," which reflects the waves into a funnel called a feed horn at the dish's middle. The waves bounce back and forth against the sides of the funnel, creating a pulse. A device called a receiver turns the pulse into an electrical signal, which travels along wires to a computer so it can be stored and studied.

TELESCOPE TALK

Some radio telescopes collect information—such as photos—sent back to Earth from space telescopes, or from probes visiting other planets. First, the space telescope or probe turns its photos into an electrical signal by converting it into a pattern of numbers—just 1s and 0s. Any information can be turned into long streams of 1s and 0s, which are the "language" used by all computers and electronic devices. A 1 turns the electrical current on, while a 0 turns it off.

The electrical signal is turned into radio waves by a device called a transmitter. Electricity flowing into the transmitter makes electrons vibrate up and down, producing radio waves. The particular pattern of the waves represents all the 1s and 0s. When the waves reach Earth, they are turned back into 1s and 0s—then into images.

Very Large Array Facts

OBJECT	Ground-based telescope
DETECTS	Radio waves
DISHES	28 telescopes with 25-m (82-ft) wide dishes
MASS	209,000 kg (460,000 lb) per telescope
SIZE	Telescopes moved along a Y shaped track, with each track arm 21 km (13 miles) long
LAUNCH	1980
LOCATION	2,124 m (6,969 ft) above sea level in New Mexico, United States

Subreflector

Dish

Feed horn

Space Telescopes

Space telescopes can detect electromagnetic radiation without it being blocked or distorted by Earth's atmosphere. The first space telescope was blasted into Earth orbit in 1961. Today, space telescopes are in orbit around both the Sun and Earth.

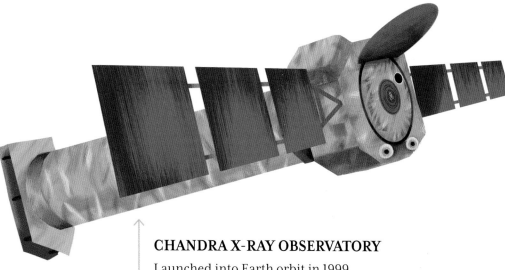

PLANCK

From 2009 to 2013, Planck studied the microwave radiation that fills space, called the cosmic microwave background. Planck's findings suggested that the Big Bang, which created this radiation, was slightly longer ago than previously thought—around 13.798 billion years.

CHANDRA X-RAY OBSERVATORY

Launched into Earth orbit in 1999, Chandra was named after astronomer Subrahmanyan Chandrasekhar. Its mirrors are made of material that reflects X-rays instead of letting them pass through, so the rays can be focused like visible light.

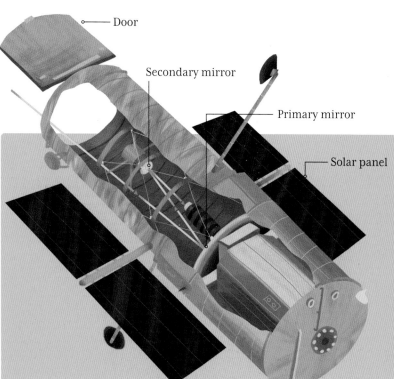

Door

Secondary mirror

Primary mirror

Solar panel

HUBBLE SPACE TELESCOPE

Hubble uses a 2.4-m (7.9-ft) primary mirror to detect mostly visible light, as well as some ultraviolet and infrared. Since being launched into Earth orbit in 1990, it has sent home more than 1 million images in the form of radio waves.

JAMES WEBB SPACE TELESCOPE

This Sun-orbiting telescope sees very faint, distant objects in infrared, allowing it to look far back in time to the very earliest galaxies and stars. A sunshade prevents the telescope warming up, so it is undisturbed by its own infrared radiation.

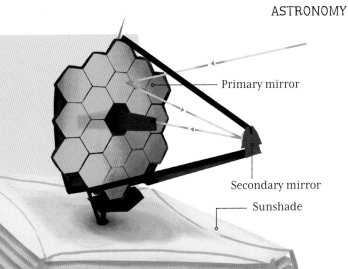

Primary mirror

Secondary mirror

Sunshade

Radio antenna

CHEOPS

CHEOPS stands for CHaracterising ExOPlanets Satellite. Launched in 2019, it focuses on nearby bright stars orbited by exoplanets. As the exoplanets pass in front of their star, it uses visible light observations to determine their size, mass, and materials.

James Webb Telescope Facts

OBJECT	Space telescope
DETECTS	Infrared and visible light
MIRRORS	3 mirrors, with a 6.5-m (21.3-ft) wide primary and 74-cm (29-in) wide secondary
MASS	6,500 kg (14,300 lb)
SIZE	21 x 14 m (69 x 46 ft)
LAUNCH	2021
LOCATION	Around 1.5 million km (1 million miles) from Earth

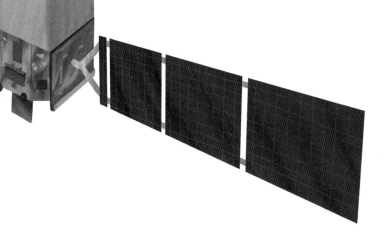

FERMI SPACE TELESCOPE

Named after the 20th-century physicist Enrico Fermi, this telescope has been observing gamma rays since 2008. It is searching for the sources of some mysterious rays, which may come from colliding galaxies or dark matter.

Exploring Space

There is no definite line between Earth's atmosphere and space, but space is said to start 100 km (62 miles) above Earth's surface. The first human-made object to reach space was a German V-2 rocket in 1944. The invention of rockets allowed the human exploration of space to begin. Rockets are powerful vehicles that can travel fast enough to overcome the pull of Earth's gravity—and fly up into space. All spacecraft are lifted into space by rockets, whether the craft carries a human crew or is an uncrewed space probe or satellite.

The farthest that humans have journeyed in space is to the far side of the Moon. This distance, around 400,171 km (248,655 miles) from Earth, was reached by the crew of the United States' Apollo 13 mission in 1970. A handful of humans have landed on or orbited the Moon, but most people who have visited space have only orbited Earth. Others have taken a suborbital flight, meaning they reached space, but did not soar high enough—at least 150 km (93 miles) above Earth's surface—to reach a stable orbit. Currently, journeying further than the Moon is difficult for humans, because of the great distances and dangerous conditions in space.

The farthest that a space probe has journeyed from Earth is more than 23.8 billion km (14.8 billion miles). That is how far *Voyager 1* is from Earth—and the probe will continue forever, unless it crashes into something, as there is little in space to slow it down. Closer to home, space probes have flown past all of the Solar System's planets. Probes have also landed on, or deliberately crashed into, Mercury, Venus, Mars, Jupiter, Saturn, our Moon, Saturn's moon Titan, five asteroids, and two comets.

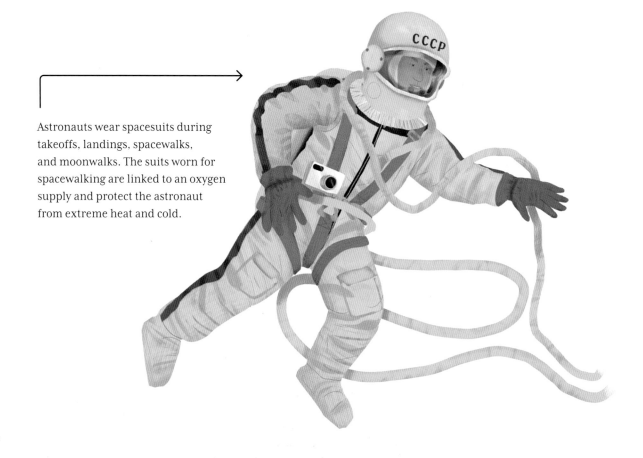

Astronauts wear spacesuits during takeoffs, landings, spacewalks, and moonwalks. The suits worn for spacewalking are linked to an oxygen supply and protect the astronaut from extreme heat and cold.

On their way to the International
Space Station in 2019, astronauts
Hazza al Mansouri, Oleg Skripochka,
and Jessica Meir are blasted into
space in a Russian Soyuz MS
spacecraft, carried by a Soyuz-FG
rocket. Astronauts always hang a
soft toy chosen by family and friends
in the Soyuz cabin. They know they
have reached space when the toy
starts to float.

Rockets

Every spacecraft needs to be lifted into space by a rocket. Once the rocket has done its job, it detaches from the spacecraft. Used rocket parts usually fall toward Earth, either burning up as they rush through the atmosphere, or splashing down safely in the ocean.

ESCAPING EARTH

A rocket needs to work against the powerful pull of Earth's gravity, the force that pulls us back to the ground when we jump. If you could jump with enough power, you would be able to jump into space! A rocket has that power. To send a space probe off to distant planets, the rocket carrying it escapes Earth's gravity by reaching "escape velocity"—a speed of at least 40,000 km/h (25,000 miles per hour).

When a rocket separates from the spacecraft it has lifted, the spacecraft continues moving at the same speed—so it heads off toward the Moon or another planet at 40,000 km/h (25,000 miles per hour). To put a satellite into orbit around Earth, a rocket has to fly less fast because the satellite's speed only needs to balance out Earth's gravity, not escape it. To launch a satellite, a rocket only has to travel at around 28,000 km/h (17,000 miles per hour).

The launch escape system has its own engine, which will fire to quickly separate the spacecraft from the rocket in an emergency.

Launch towers, containing an elevator for the astronauts, are pulled back.

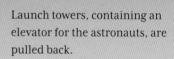

Soyuz-FG Facts

OBJECT	Rocket
MASS	305,000 kg (672,000 lb)
HEIGHT	49.5 m (162.4 ft)
USED	2001–2019
COUNTRY	Russia
LAUNCHES	70
LAUNCH PAD	Baikonur Cosmodrome, Kazakhstan

HOW ROCKETS WORK

To reach such immense speeds, a rocket's engines burn a lot of fuel, up to 5,000 kg (11,000 lb) per second. This creates a downward blast of hot gas, which pushes the rocket upward in reaction. You can experience a similar effect when you kick backward against the wall of a swimming pool—which creates the reaction of you surging off across the pool!

These actions and reactions are all explained by the third law of motion, which was figured out in 1686 by British scientist Isaac Newton. The law tells us that for every action, there is always an equal and opposite reaction.

Due to the weight of all the fuel needed to lift a rocket into space, rockets have up to five parts, named stages. Each stage has its own fuel tanks and engines. Each stage burns its fuel in turn. Once a stage has used up its fuel, it detaches so that the remaining stages can fly faster without having to carry the weight of the empty fuel tanks and engines.

The Soyuz-FG rocket has three stages. Once in space, after the three stages have fallen away, the protective fairing opens to release the Soyuz spacecraft.

Launch escape system

Fairing

Soyuz MS spacecraft

Third stage

Second stage

The Soyuz-FG rocket blasts off, carrying a Soyuz MS spacecraft.

First stage

Crewed Spacecraft

There are two types of spacecraft that carry astronauts—space capsules and spaceplanes.
Nearly all have been capsules, which fall to Earth—slowed by parachutes—after their mission.
Spaceplanes have wings, so they land on a runway like an ordinary airplane.

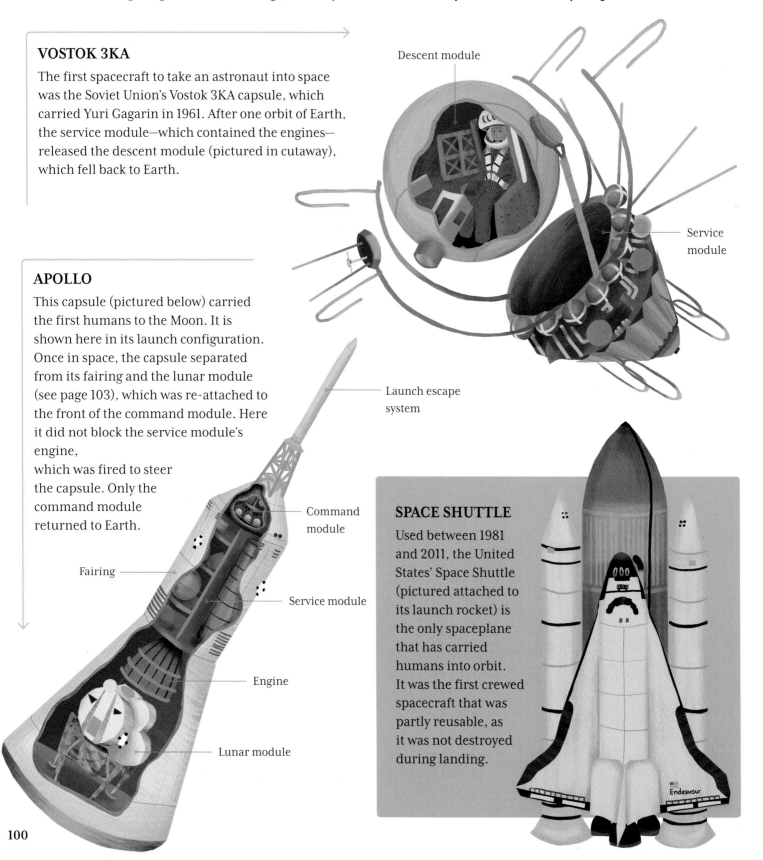

VOSTOK 3KA

The first spacecraft to take an astronaut into space was the Soviet Union's Vostok 3KA capsule, which carried Yuri Gagarin in 1961. After one orbit of Earth, the service module—which contained the engines—released the descent module (pictured in cutaway), which fell back to Earth.

Descent module

Service module

APOLLO

This capsule (pictured below) carried the first humans to the Moon. It is shown here in its launch configuration. Once in space, the capsule separated from its fairing and the lunar module (see page 103), which was re-attached to the front of the command module. Here it did not block the service module's engine, which was fired to steer the capsule. Only the command module returned to Earth.

Launch escape system

Fairing

Command module

Service module

Engine

Lunar module

SPACE SHUTTLE

Used between 1981 and 2011, the United States' Space Shuttle (pictured attached to its launch rocket) is the only spaceplane that has carried humans into orbit. It was the first crewed spacecraft that was partly reusable, as it was not destroyed during landing.

Endeavour

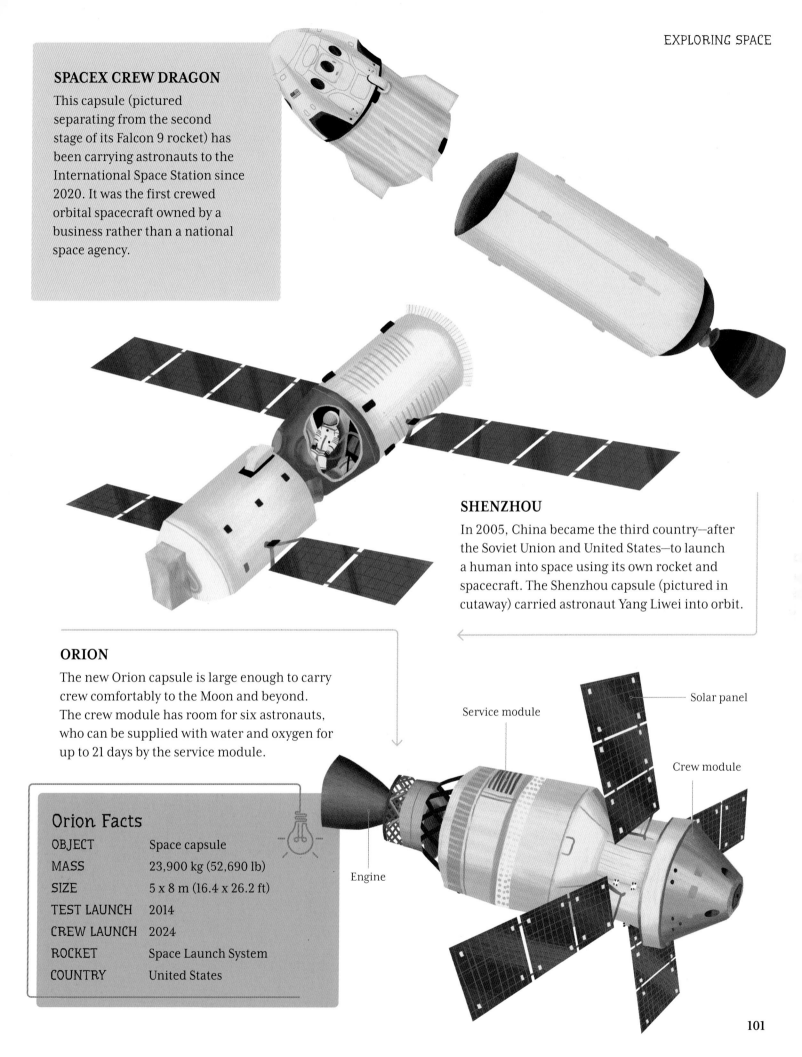

SPACEX CREW DRAGON

This capsule (pictured separating from the second stage of its Falcon 9 rocket) has been carrying astronauts to the International Space Station since 2020. It was the first crewed orbital spacecraft owned by a business rather than a national space agency.

SHENZHOU

In 2005, China became the third country—after the Soviet Union and United States—to launch a human into space using its own rocket and spacecraft. The Shenzhou capsule (pictured in cutaway) carried astronaut Yang Liwei into orbit.

ORION

The new Orion capsule is large enough to carry crew comfortably to the Moon and beyond. The crew module has room for six astronauts, who can be supplied with water and oxygen for up to 21 days by the service module.

Solar panel

Service module

Crew module

Engine

Orion Facts

OBJECT	Space capsule
MASS	23,900 kg (52,690 lb)
SIZE	5 x 8 m (16.4 x 26.2 ft)
TEST LAUNCH	2014
CREW LAUNCH	2024
ROCKET	Space Launch System
COUNTRY	United States

Landing on the Moon

The first people to walk on the Moon were US astronauts Neil Armstrong and Edwin "Buzz" Aldrin, on July 21, 1969, during the Apollo 11 mission. From launch to splashdown, the mission lasted 8 days, 3 hours, and 18 minutes.

The mission began when three astronauts—Armstrong, Aldrin, and Michael Collins—lifted off from Kennedy Space Center, in Florida, on July 16. Their Apollo space capsule (see page 100) was launched by a Saturn V rocket. After separating from the rocket, the capsule journeyed for 3 days until—by firing the engine to adjust course—it moved into orbit around the Moon. On July 20, Armstrong and Aldrin transferred from the capsule's command and service module into the lunar module, which Armstrong flew down to the Moon. Collins stayed in the command module to make sure the others could return safely.

Armstrong and Aldrin stayed on the Moon for just over 21 hours, but spent only 2 hours and 31 minutes walking on the surface. For the remainder of the time, they prepared and rested in the lunar module. At the end of their visit, they flew the lunar module back up to the command and service module, which the astronauts steered toward Earth. Once they had entered Earth orbit, the engine-carrying service module was separated from the command module, which splashed down in the Pacific Ocean on July 24. Floats stopped the module from sinking, while the astronauts were rescued by the US navy.

NEIL ARMSTRONG

Armstrong was the first to step onto the Moon, saying the famous words "One small step for [a] man, one giant leap for mankind." As the pair explored, Armstrong took most of the photos using a camera attached to his spacesuit.

STARS AND STRIPES

The astronauts planted a US flag, which fell over when the lunar module lifted off. Since there is little atmosphere—and no wind—on the Moon, the flag had a bar across the top so it looked as if it was fluttering in the photos.

LUNAR MODULE

The lunar module was nicknamed *Eagle*. A TV camera was mounted on it, so images of the astronauts' first steps were watched, almost live, by 600 million people. After *Eagle* had been flown back to the command and service module, it was left in Moon orbit.

TRANQUILITY BASE

When the lunar module landed in the Moon's Sea of Tranquility, the astronauts named the spot *Tranquility Base*. In 1970, three small craters to the north of the base were named Aldrin, Collins, and Armstrong.

EXPERIMENTS PACKAGE

A pack of scientific equipment included a device to measure moonquakes. Aldrin also hammered a metal tube into the Moon's surface to take a rock sample, while both men scooped dust into bags.

BUZZ ALDRIN

Aldrin experimented with methods of getting around in the Moon's low gravity (since it has less mass than Earth). He tried two-footed kangaroo hops but preferred bounding strides. Aldrin became the first to pee on the Moon, which he did into a bag inside his spacesuit.

Satellites

Artificial satellites are human-made objects that are placed in orbit around Earth or another space object. There are currently more than 8,000 satellites orbiting Earth. They carry out many different jobs, from communication to weather-watching.

SPUTNIK 1

The first satellite was the Soviet Union's *Sputnik 1*, which orbited Earth from October 1957 to January 1958. Like all satellites, it stayed in orbit because the pull of Earth's gravity was balanced by its speed, which was given by the rocket that lifted it. However, as *Sputnik 1* pushed against Earth's outer atmosphere, it slowed down, making it fall and burn up.

GPS III

This Global Positioning System (GPS) satellite helps people find their way. A phone or other satellite navigation device receives radio signals from several GPS satellites, each signal stating the time it left the satellite and the satellite's location. Since radio waves travel at a set speed, the device can calculate its distance to all the satellites—and figure out where it is.

TELSTAR 1

Launched in 1962, this US communications satellite bounced the first live television images between the United States and Europe. The satellite received and sent the images as radio waves (see page 93).

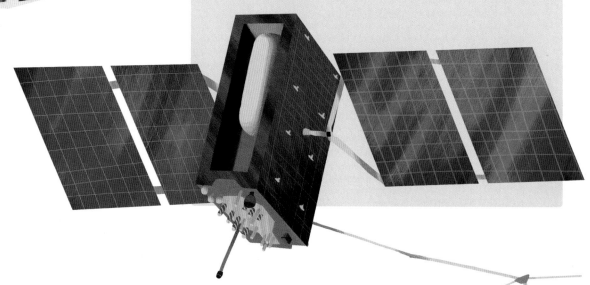

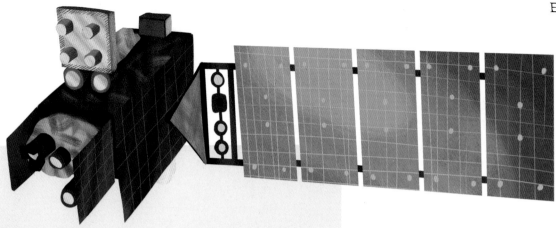

GOES-18

Powered by its solar panels, this weather satellite watches Earth's clouds and smoke. The information it collects is used to give warnings of storms, flooding, and wildfires.

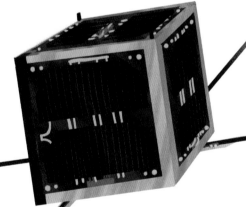

GRACE-FO

Since 2019, these twin satellites have been measuring the pull of Earth's gravity, which varies slightly across its surface depending on whether there is rock, water, or ice. The satellites shoot microwaves at each other to detect changes, caused by gravity, in the other satellite's speed and height.

FUNCUBE-1

FUNcube-1 was the first satellite launched only for the use of schoolchildren. It is a type of mini, inexpensive satellite known as a CubeSat. Radio receivers in schools can pick up temperature information from the satellite as it moves in and out of sunlight.

FUNcube-1 Facts

OBJECT	Educational CubeSat
MASS	0.98 kg (2.2 lb)
SIZE	10 x 10 cm (4 x 4 in)
LAUNCH	2013
COUNTRY	United Kingdom
INSTRUMENTS	Temperature sensors and radio antenna
LOCATION	Around 636 km (395 miles) above Earth

International Space Station

A space station is a satellite large enough for astronauts to live on. Around 109 m (358 ft) long and 73 m (240 ft) wide, the International Space Station (ISS) is the largest space station in orbit around Earth. Since 2000, it has been lived in by changing crews of astronauts from around the world.

The ISS holds a crew of seven astronauts, who carry out experiments in the station's "microgravity" environment. Microgravity makes people and objects seem to be weightless. Yet Earth's gravity is pulling on the ISS almost as much as if it were on Earth. In fact, the ISS and its astronauts are all falling due to the pull of Earth's gravity. The ISS's high speed (which "tries" to make the station travel away from Earth) balances the pull of gravity, making the ISS's fall curved—so it orbits around Earth. As the space station and astronauts fall around Earth together, the astronauts seem to float.

The ISS orbits around 415 km (258 miles) above Earth's surface, making 15.5 orbits every day. Due to the effort of pushing through the high atmosphere, the ISS would gradually slow and drop from this orbit if the engines on the Zvezda module were not regularly fired. In this way, the ISS maintains a speed of around 28,000 km/h (17,000 miles per hour).

SOLAR PANELS

Solar panels up to 34 m (112 ft) long supply the ISS with electricity. This powers the computers, lighting, and recycling system, which cleans waste water from the two toilets. This water is used for drinking and to make oxygen for breathing, by splitting it into its parts—hydrogen and oxygen.

COLUMBUS MODULE

Astronauts in this Europe-run laboratory (pictured in cutaway) carry out experiments on plants and small invertebrates, such as ants, to see how microgravity affects them. One day, the results could help us take plants and animals to Mars.

ZVEZDA MODULE

Workplace of the Russian crew, Zvezda is also the dock for crew-carrying Soyuz spacecraft and food-carrying Progress spacecraft. Zvezda has sleeping compartments for two Russian astronauts, and a toilet to which astronauts must strap themselves.

CANADARM2

This 17-m (55.8-ft) robotic arm—which can slide along the outside of the ISS—is used to move supplies. It also helped spacewalking astronauts to construct the ISS modules from their ready-made parts while in orbit.

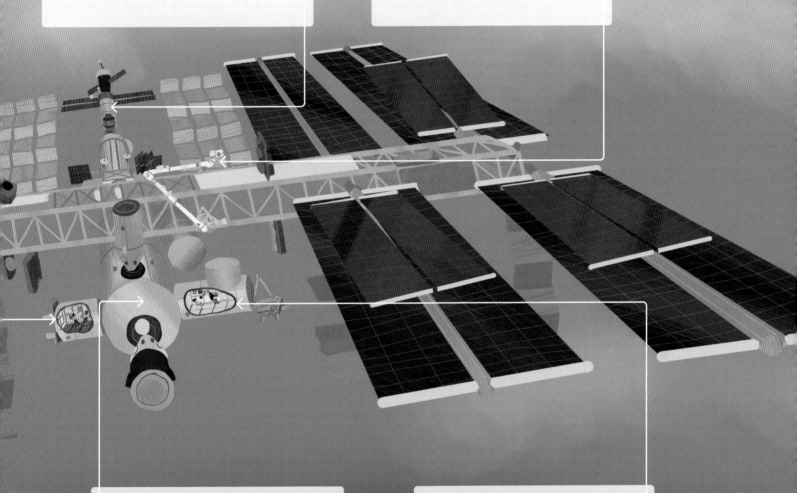

HARMONY MODULE

This module has four sleeping compartments, where crew members lie in a loosely strapped sleeping bag. Harmony connects the laboratory modules of the United States, Europe, and Japan. It is also a dock for SpaceX Crew Dragons and Cygnus

KIBŌ MODULE

Completed in 2009, this is the Japanese laboratory (pictured in cutaway), but it is shared by astronauts from many countries. Its 15.2-m (49.9-ft) length makes it the largest ISS module.

Space Probes

Space probes are spacecraft with no human crew. There are four main types—flyby probes, which fly past space objects while taking photos and collecting information; orbiters, which orbit space objects; landers, which touch down on them; and rovers, which travel across them.

VENERA 7

When this probe landed on Venus in 1970, it was the first spacecraft to soft land on (rather than crash into) another planet. It was also the first to send information—including Venus's 475 °C (887 °F) temperature—from another planet, which it did using radio waves.

LUNOKHOD 1

Carried to the Moon by the Soviet Union's *Luna 17* spacecraft in 1970, *Lunokhod 1* was the first rover to travel across another space object. Its equipment included radio transmitters, cameras, and an X-ray telescope.

MARINER 9

The first successful orbiter was the USA's *Mariner 9*. Supplied with electricity by its four solar panels, it sent 7,329 images of Mars back to Earth between November 1971 and October 1972.

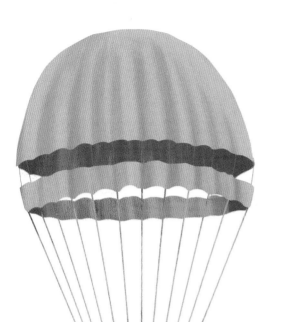

VOYAGER 1

This probe flew past Jupiter, Saturn, and several of their moons, before leaving the Solar System in 2012. It is the most distant human-made object from Earth—and is still sending home information.

HUYGENS

In December 2004, the *Cassini* orbiter released the *Huygens* lander, which soft landed—with the help of a parachute—on Saturn's moon Titan in January 2005. This was the most distant landing from Earth ever made by a spacecraft.

Voyager 1 Facts

OBJECT	Flyby probe
MASS	722 kg (1,592 lb)
SIZE	13 x 3.7 m (42.7 x 12 ft)
LAUNCH	1977
COUNTRY	United States
INSTRUMENTS	Cameras, radio telescope, and infrared, ultraviolet, and magnetic field detectors (some instruments no longer working)
LOCATION	Over 23.8 billion km (14.8 billion miles) from Earth

Sample collector

STARDUST

Stardust was the first spacecraft to return material from a comet. The probe caught dust from the comet Wild 2 using its sample collector, which was then pulled back into a capsule that landed in the US desert in 2006.

Exploring Mars

After the Moon, Mars is the space object we have explored most, by using more than 40 space probes. Although humans have not yet landed on Mars, it is the only planet where we have used rovers to travel across the surface in our place.

WHY MARS?

Mars has been explored more than other planets and their moons, because—although its current lack of a breathable atmosphere and liquid water make it unsuitable for life— it is suitable for robotic space probes. Unlike the outer planets, it has a solid surface. Unlike the other inner planets, Mercury and Venus, it is not so hot that machines cannot work for long.

In addition, Mars's history (see page 36) suggests it could once have been suitable for life. Astronomers are eager to see if space probes can find signs of ancient tiny life forms there. Some moons of the outer planets (such as Jupiter's Ganymede and Saturn's Titan) may also be suitable for life, but Mars's location makes it easier to reach. At the planet's closest approach to Earth, the journey is only 7 months, while the voyage to Titan is around 7 years.

Perseverance has an arm 2.1 m (6.9 ft) long that drills into the surface, then stores rock samples in tubes that might be picked up by a future mission.

MOVING ALONG

The first rover on Mars was the United States' *Sojourner*, in 1997. *Sojourner* was delivered to Mars by the lander *Mars Pathfinder*, which opened to release the rover once on the ground. Unlike later rovers, *Sojourner* was small and lightweight—just 28 cm (11 in) high and 10.6 kg (23 lb). No one was sure it would survive on Mars. However, over 85 days, it managed to roll 100 m (328 ft) on its six metal wheels. Once a day, the rover's computer received a series of commands, sent by radio waves from an Earth-based driver. Before communication was lost, the rover's cameras sent home fuzzy images of rocks and sand.

Since *Sojourner*, five other rovers have worked successfully on Mars, four from the United States and one from China. In 2021, the United States' *Perseverance* rover started to roll across Mars's Jezero Crater with support from its mini-helicopter, *Ingenuity* (nicknamed *Ginny*).

Perseverance searches for signs of past life, and tests the soil and atmosphere. One of its instruments separates small amounts of oxygen from carbon dioxide (which is made of carbon and oxygen) in the Martian atmosphere. The results of this experiment could help with supplying oxygen for breathing on human missions to Mars.

Ingenuity made the first powered flight on another planet on April 19, 2021. Its job is to spot suitable areas for *Perseverance* to investigate.

Perseverance Facts

OBJECT	Rover
MASS	1,025 kg (2,260 lb)
SIZE	2.9 x 2.7 m (9.5 x 8.9 ft)
LAUNCH	2020
COUNTRY	United States
INSTRUMENTS	19 cameras, 2 microphones, and 7 instruments, including spectrometers (which analyze materials), and sensors that measure temperature and wind speed
LOCATION	Jezero Crater, Mars

Astronaut Training

An astronaut's training can take up to five years. The training prepares them for the physical and mental challenges of space travel. They are taught how to operate their spacecraft and scientific equipment.

SPACE SICKNESS

Around three-quarters of astronauts experience space motion sickness during the first days of a flight and while landing. Similar to the motion sickness that some people experience in cars, it causes dizziness and vomiting. Space sickness is due to changes in speed, direction, and gravity, which confuse the astronaut's sense of balance.

To help master motion sickness, trainees spend time in a microgravity environment (see page 106). An ordinary plane (nicknamed a "vomit comet") flies them steeply into the sky, then dives steeply, creating 25 seconds of floating "weightlessness" as it plunges—similar to the feeling on a plummeting rollercoaster. However, since vomiting inside a helmet is messy and unsafe, astronauts also take medication for launches and landings.

LEARNING TO FLY

Trainee astronauts learn to fly their spacecraft by working in life-size, ground-based copies of the craft. Even astronauts who will not be piloting the craft take this training in case of emergency. Astronauts learn to operate the controls in the cockpit, how to dock the craft with a space station, and how to use communication equipment.

A key skill for trainees to learn is opening and closing airlocks. An airlock is a compartment on a spacecraft with two sets of doors, with the outer doors opening onto airless space. When the outer door is opened so an astronaut can spacewalk, the inner door must be shut so astronauts in the craft can continue to breathe air. Once the outer door is closed again, air is pumped into the compartment before the inner door is opened.

STAYING HAPPY

Trainees are also given advice about avoiding arguments with other astronauts when they are together on a cramped spacecraft for days or weeks. They are given tips on how to relax, how to think calming thoughts, and how to work well with their team. Astronauts heading for a space station are reminded to take time every day to exercise, play games, watch movies, listen to music, read books, and talk to their families.

Trainees use virtual reality computer programs to feel as if they are piloting a spacecraft or operating a robotic arm. Sensors respond to the trainee's movements, while the headset shows a changing view.

Trainee astronauts prepare for spacewalks underwater, which gives a similar floating sensation. They work with copies of the tools that they will use to repair a space station or telescope in space.

113

Astronauts

More than 600 people have reached space, earning themselves the name "astronaut." Astronauts are usually paid by a government space agency, but since 2001, some have been unpaid tourists or commercial astronauts, who are paid by businesses.

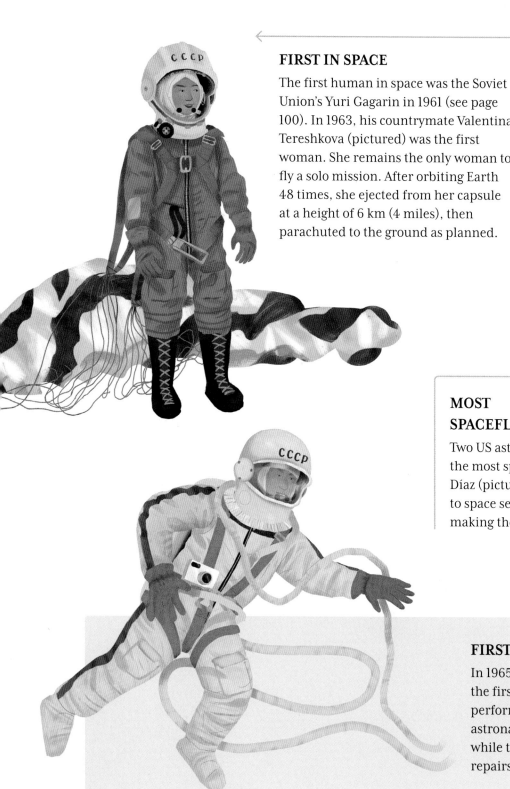

FIRST IN SPACE

The first human in space was the Soviet Union's Yuri Gagarin in 1961 (see page 100). In 1963, his countrymate Valentina Tereshkova (pictured) was the first woman. She remains the only woman to fly a solo mission. After orbiting Earth 48 times, she ejected from her capsule at a height of 6 km (4 miles), then parachuted to the ground as planned.

MOST SPACEFLIGHTS

Two US astronauts share the record for the most spaceflights. Franklin Chang-Díaz (pictured) and Jerry Ross both went to space seven times on Space Shuttles, making their last flights in 2002.

FIRST SPACEWALK

In 1965, the Soviet Union's Alexei Leonov was the first person to exit their spacecraft and perform a spacewalk. During spacewalks, astronauts are usually tethered to their craft while they carry out experiments or make repairs to a space station.

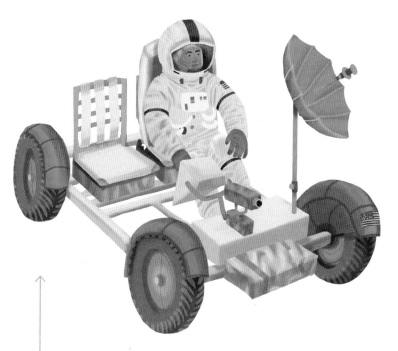

Moon Walker Facts

1969	Apollo 11: Neil Armstrong and Buzz Aldrin
1969	Apollo 12: Charles "Pete" Conrad and Alan Bean
1971	Apollo 14: Alan Shepard and Edgar Mitchell
1971	Apollo 15: David Scott and James Irwin
1972	Apollo 16: John Young and Charles Duke
1972	Apollo 17: Gene Cernan and Harrison Schmitt

MOON WALKERS

Only 12 people have walked on the Moon, all of them men from the United States. The first was Neil Armstrong (see page 102), while the last was Gene Cernan (pictured), who spent a record-breaking 74 hours and 59 minutes on the Moon.

COMMANDERS OF THE ISS

The first commander of the International Space Station was the USA's William Shepherd in 2001. The first female commander was the USA's Peggy Whitson (pictured) in 2007. She commanded it again in 2017. Whitson has spent 675 days in space, more than any other woman.

COMMERCIAL ASTRONAUTS

In 2021, pilot Sian Proctor (pictured left) flew the first orbital commercial spaceflight carrying only space tourists. On board the SpaceX-owned Crew Dragon was Hayley Arceneaux (pictured right), the first person in space with a prosthetic leg bone after surviving bone cancer as a child.

Humans on Mars

The space agencies of Europe, Russia, and the United States have plans to send humans to Mars within the next 20 or 30 years. One day, they hope to build a permanent base there, where astronauts can live and work.

The United States has already taken a step toward the goal of sending humans to Mars. It has built its large Orion space capsule (see page 101), which could be attached to an even larger Deep Space Habitat to house a crew for the months-long journey. Along with Canada, Europe, and Japan, the United States is currently taking the next step in its plan—setting up a space station in orbit around the Moon, called the Lunar Gateway. This station will be a dock for landers carrying astronauts to and from the Moon's surface. Within a few years, those astronauts will construct a base on the Moon itself.

Astronauts staying on the Moon base will test the techniques needed for a base on Mars, which would be supported by a similar Mars-orbiting space station. A Mars base would need to supply its own oxygen, water, and food. In addition, the fuel to power a spacecraft for the long journey home would be too heavy to carry to Mars, so would have to be made on the planet. Here's how a Mars base might look …

GREENHOUSE

Plants are grown from seeds brought from Earth. Since Mars is cold and its sunlight weak, they are in a heated greenhouse with lights that mimic sunlight. The plants use this light to make their own food from water and carbon dioxide, which is found in the Martian atmosphere.

MANUFACTURING MODULES

Water is made by heating the soil until its ice evaporates (turns to gas), then condensing it into liquid. Oxygen for breathing is taken from the water, by splitting it into its parts— oxygen and hydrogen. Fuel for landers and rovers is made from oxygen, hydrogen, and carbon, which is also found on the planet.

MARS LANDER

An immense lander carries astronauts, vehicles, materials, and supplies between the surface of Mars and an orbiting space station. The lander is coated in super-strong materials, such as carbon fiber, that are not damaged by the heat of takeoff and landing.

SOLAR PANELS

Solar panels make electricity from sunlight to power all the base's modules. Some power is stored for use at night and during dust storms, which often cover the panels in sand.

HABITATION MODULES

Modules where astronauts sleep are built on Mars using 3D printing. On Earth, 3D printers make objects by squirting molten plastic from a nozzle. On Mars, a rover-sized printing machine melts and squirts out material found on the planet, such as the rock basalt.

Questions and Answers

WHEN WERE THE SOLAR SYSTEM'S SEVEN OTHER PLANETS DISCOVERED?

Mercury, Venus, Mars, Jupiter, and Saturn have been known since ancient times because they can be seen with the naked eye as bright, moving lights. Although Uranus can be seen dimly with the naked eye, it was not considered to be a planet until 1781, when astronomer William Herschel viewed it through his telescope. Neptune was spotted in 1846, when German astronomer Johann Galle found it through a telescope, after its suspected location was pinpointed by mathematicians and astronomers.

WHICH IS THE SOLAR SYSTEM'S LARGEST MOON?

The largest moon is Jupiter's Ganymede, which is 5,268 km (3,273 miles) across. The second largest is Saturn's Titan, followed by Jupiter's Callisto and Io. Earth's Moon is in fifth place, followed by Jupiter's Europa, Neptune's Triton, Uranus's Titania, and Saturn's Rhea. In tenth place is Uranus's Oberon, which is 1,523 km (946 miles) wide.

Ganymede

Pluto and its five moons

WHICH IS THE BIGGEST DWARF PLANET IN THE SOLAR SYSTEM?

At 2,376 km (1,476 miles) across, Pluto is the widest dwarf planet. However, it has slightly less mass than Eris, the second widest dwarf planet at 2,326 km (1,445 miles) across. Until 2006, when the International Astronomical Union redefined planets and dwarf planets, Pluto was classified as a planet.

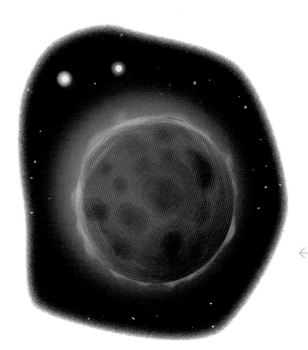

WHICH STAR IS CLOSEST TO THE SUN?

The nearest star to the Sun is Proxima Centauri, around 4.2 light-years away in the constellation of Centaurus. It is part of a triple star system, in which three stars orbit each other. The other two stars, Alpha Centauri A and B, are more than 4.3 light-years away from the Sun.

HOW OLD IS THE MILKY WAY?

Astronomers estimate that the Milky Way is around 13.6 billion years old, having started to form not long after the Universe was born around 13.8 billion years ago. The Sun, which lies 28,000 light-years from the middle of the Milky Way, did not form until 4.6 billion years ago, soon followed by its planets.

The Local Group of galaxies

HOW MANY STARS ARE IN THE UNIVERSE?

Astronomers estimate that there are 1 septillion (1 followed by 24 zeros) stars in the Universe. This estimate is based on the number of stars in known galaxies, multiplied by the number of galaxies that might be in the observable Universe. There are at least 100 billion stars in the Milky Way, while there may be 2 trillion galaxies.

WHAT ARE THE BRIGHTEST OBJECTS IN THE UNIVERSE?

Quasars are the Universe's brightest objects, emitting more light than all the stars in the Milky Way put together. "Quasar" is the name for the region at the heart of young galaxy where a very active black hole is sucking in material. As material circles the black hole, it gets so hot it emits jets of light and other forms of electromagnetic radiation.

Timeline of Exploration

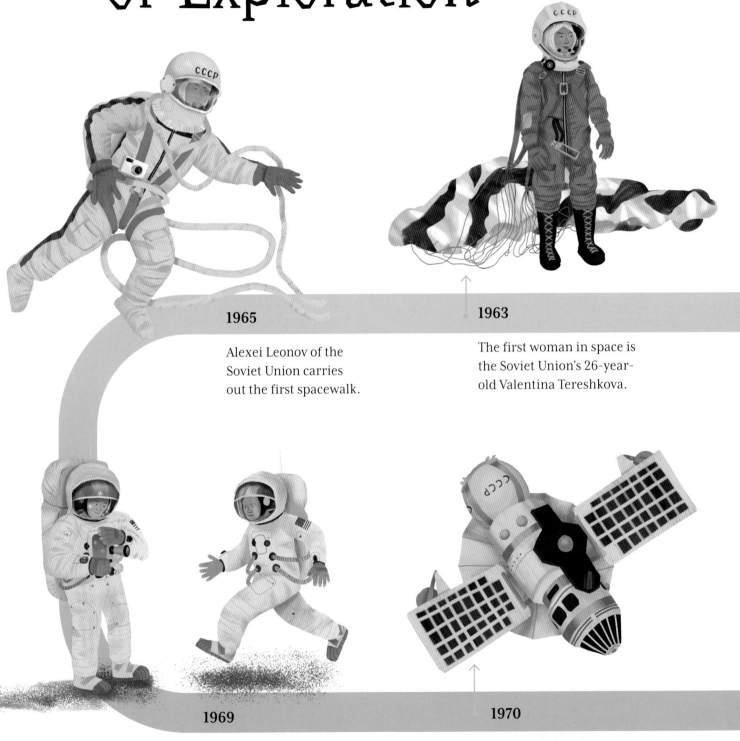

1965

Alexei Leonov of the Soviet Union carries out the first spacewalk.

1963

The first woman in space is the Soviet Union's 26-year-old Valentina Tereshkova.

1969

US astronauts Neil Armstrong and Edwin "Buzz" Aldrin become the first humans to walk on the Moon during the Apollo 11 mission.

1970

Venera 7, belonging to the Soviet Union, is the first space probe to soft land on another planet.

1944

The German V-2 rocket is the first human-made object to reach space.

1957

The first successful satellite, the Soviet Union's *Sputnik 1*, goes into orbit around Earth.

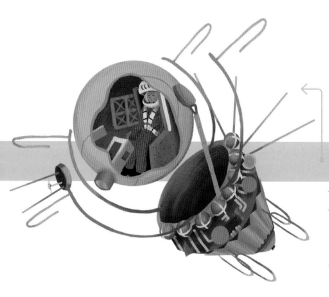

1961

When the Soviet Union's Yuri Gagarin makes one orbit of Earth in a Vostok 3KA space capsule, he becomes the first human in space.

1959

The first photos of Earth from orbit are taken by the United States' satellite *Explorer 6*.

1970

When it rolls across the Moon, the Soviet Union's *Lunokhod 1* is the first rover to travel on another space object.

1971

The Soviet Union's *Salyut 1* is the first space station to orbit Earth.

1989

The United States' *Voyager 2* is the first probe to fly past the most distant planet, Neptune.

1982

The Soviet Union's *Venera 13* probe makes the first sound recording on another planet—Venus.

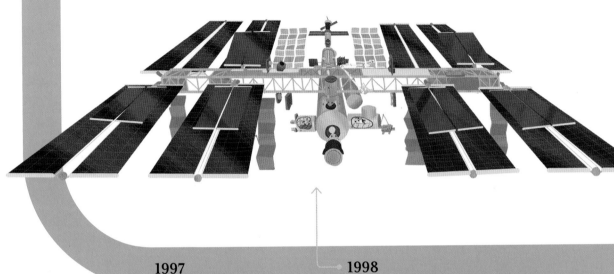

1997

The United States' *Sojourner* is the first rover to travel across another planet—Mars.

1998

The first modules of the International Space Station are launched. It becomes the longest-serving and largest space station.

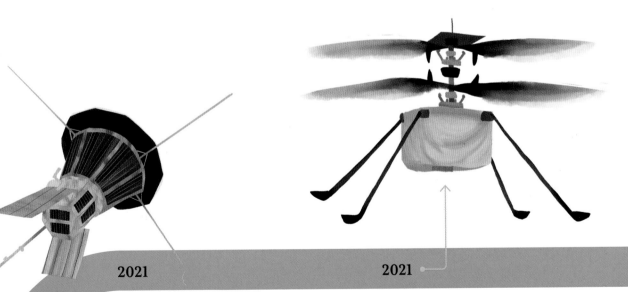

2021

The United States' *Parker Soler Probe* is the first to fly through the atmosphere of the Sun.

2021

When it buzzes over the Martian surface, the United States' mini-helicopter *Ingenuity* is the first probe to make a powered flight on another planet.

1981

The United States' Space Shuttle is the first partly reusable spaceplane to lift humans into orbit.

1971

When it reaches Mars, the United States' *Mariner 9* is the first probe to orbit another planet.

2001

The United States' *NEAR Shoemaker* probe is the first to land on an asteroid, named Eros.

2006

The first dust from a comet, sampled from Wild 2 by the United States' *Stardust* probe, is returned to Earth.

2019

Seeds carried on the Chinese Moon lander *Chang'e 4* start to grow on the Moon in a sealed container.

2012

Voyager 1 becomes the first human-made object to leave the Solar System.

Glossary

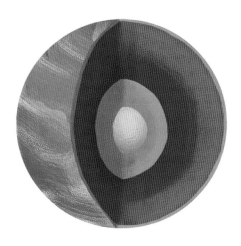

active galactic nucleus
The area at the middle of a young galaxy that gives off immense radiation, caused by material circling a supermassive black hole.

asterism
A pattern or group of stars inside one of the official constellations.

asteroid
A small rocky or metal object that orbits the Sun.

astronomer
A scientist who studies planets, stars, and space itself.

atmosphere
The gases surrounding a planet, moon, star, or other space object, held by its gravity.

atom
The smallest building block of matter. An atom has a central nucleus, containing particles called protons and neutrons, usually surrounded by one or more electrons.

aurora
Lights in the sky made by particles from the Sun exciting gases in the atmosphere.

axis
An imaginary line through the middle of a planet, moon, star, or other space object, around which the object rotates.

black hole
An area of space with such strong gravity that not even light can escape from it.

blazar
An area at the core of a galaxy that gives off powerful jets of energy in the direction of Earth.

carbon dioxide
A substance made of carbon and oxygen atoms. Carbon dioxide is a gas at room temperature.

chromosphere
An inner layer of the Sun's atmosphere.

comet
A small icy object with an elliptical (like a stretched circle) orbit that takes it both close to and far from the Sun.

command module
The section of a space capsule, such as the Apollo or Orion capsule, that holds the crew. It is the only part that returns to Earth.

constellation
A group of stars that seem to make a shape in the night sky.

convection zone
A layer of a star where photons move through a process called convection. They are carried by currents of hot plasma, which rise, cool, then sink.

core
The inner region of a planet, moon, star, or other space object.

corona
The outer layer of the Sun's atmosphere.

counterclockwise
Also known as anticlockwise; the opposite direction from the way the hands of a clock turn.

crust
The outer layer of a planet or moon.

dense
Tightly packed.

dwarf planet
An object orbiting a star that is massive enough for its gravity to pull it into a ball-like shape, but is not massive enough to clear other objects out of its path.

dwarf star
A star of average or low brightness and size.

eclipse
When an object such as a star, planet, or moon passes into the shadow of—or passes behind—another body.

electric charge
A property of electrons and protons, which are particles found in atoms. Electricity is a flow of electrically charged particles.

electromagnetic radiation
A type of energy that travels at the speed of light. Radiations are given different names depending on the amount of energy they carry, from low-energy radio waves, through microwaves, infrared, visible light, ultraviolet, and X-rays, to the highest-energy gamma rays.

electron
A particle found in atoms, outside the nucleus. Electricity is mostly driven by the flow of electrons from one place to another.

ellipse
An oval shape.

equator
An imaginary line drawn around a planet or star, halfway between its poles, dividing it into northern and southern halves.

exoplanet
A planet that lies outside our Solar System; also known as an extrasolar planet.

fairing
Also known as a nose cone, a fairing is a protective covering—shaped like a cone and cylinder—that encloses a space capsule or satellite while it is being lifted by a rocket. Once outside Earth's atmosphere, the fairing separates and is abandoned.

galaxy
Millions or trillions of stars, as well as gas and dust, all held together by gravity.

gas
A substance, such as air, that can move freely and has no fixed shape.

gas giant
A large planet made mostly of swirling hydrogen and helium, which are gasses at room temperature on Earth.

gravity
A force that pulls all objects toward each other. The greater an object's mass, the greater the pull of its gravity.

helium
The second most common and second lightest atom in the Universe. Helium is a gas at room temperature.

hemisphere
Half of a sphere, such as a planet or moon.

hydrogen
The most common and lightest atom in the Universe. Hydrogen is a gas at room temperature.

ice giant
A large planet made mostly of swirling water, ammonia, and methane, which scientists call "ices."

impact crater
A bowl-shaped dip on a planet or moon caused by a collision with an asteroid or other object.

infinite
Endless in size or number.

infrared
A type of energy that humans can feel as heat.

lava
Melted rock that has spilled from a volcano.

light-year
The distance light travels in 1 year—9.46 trillion km (5.88 trillion miles).

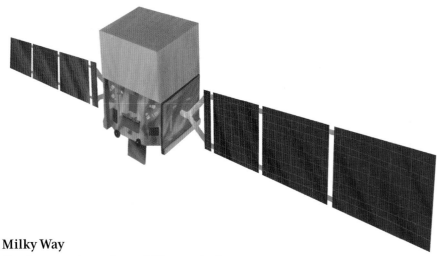

magma
Melted rock beneath the surface of a planet or moon.

magnetism
A force caused by the movement of electric charge, resulting in pulling and pushing forces between objects.

mantle
A layer inside a planet or moon that lies between the core and crust.

mass
A measure of the amount of matter in an object; often called "weight."

matter
A physical substance, in the form of a solid, liquid, gas, or plasma.

metal
A solid material that is usually hard, shiny, and bendy. Metals include iron, nickel, and gold.

meteor
A streak of light in the sky, caused by a space object burning up in Earth's atmosphere.

meteorite
A space object that has fallen to Earth's surface.

methane
A substance made of hydrogen and carbon atoms. Methane is a gas at room temperature on Earth.

Milky Way
Our home galaxy, shaped like a spiral with a bar across its core.

molecule
A group of atoms that are bonded together.

moon
A rounded object orbiting a planet.

naked eye
Human sight, without the help of a telescope or other device.

neutron star
The core of a supermassive star, left behind by a supernova explosion.

orbit
The curved path of an object around a star, planet, or moon.

oxygen
The third most common atom. Oxygen is a gas at room temperature, and is essential for life.

particle
A tiny portion of matter.

penumbra
A part of a shadow in which only some of the light is blocked. The penumbra of a sunspot is its warmer outer region.

photon
A particle that carries energy.

photosphere
The visible "surface" of the Sun.

planet
An object orbiting a star that is massive enough for its gravity to pull it into a ball-like shape and to remove other large objects from its path.

plasma
An electrically charged gas made of free electrons and atoms that have lost electrons.

pole
The far north or far south point where a planet's axis meets its surface.

proton
A particle found in atoms, located inside the nucleus.

pulsar
A fast-spinning neutron star with an intense magnetic field that forces its radiation into two beams.

radiation zone
A layer of a star where photons move by a process called radiation. They bounce from atom to atom.

radio wave
A type of energy that can be used for sending information. The information is "coded" into a radio wave by changing the wave's shape.

ring system
A plate-like or ring-like disk of material—including dust, ice, and moonlets—that orbits a planet's equator.

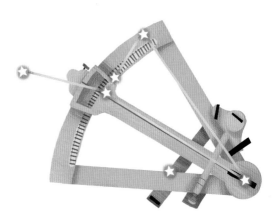

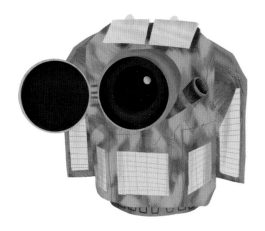

rock
A solid material made of a mixture of minerals, which are themselves made of atoms such as oxygen and silicon.

Roman numerals
A system developed in ancient Rome that uses letters to represent numbers.

room temperature
A comfortable indoor temperature.

rotation
Turning around an axis.

service module
The uninhabited portion of a space capsule that holds machines and fuel tanks. At the end of the mission, the service module separates from the command module and usually burns up in Earth's atmosphere.

solar panel
A device that turns sunlight into electricity.

Solar System
The Sun and all the objects, from planets to asteroids, that are orbiting it.

Soviet Union
A country that, from 1922 to 1991, included Russia and surrounding nations.

space capsule
A wingless spacecraft.

space probe
An uncrewed spacecraft that explores the Solar System and beyond, while sending back signals to Earth.

space telescope
A telescope that orbits in space so it is not affected by Earth's atmosphere.

spectrum
The spread-out band of visible light with different shades—from red to violet—created by passing light through a prism or similar device, as well as the whole range of invisible electromagnetic radiation, from radio waves to gamma rays.

sphere
A ball-shaped object.

star
A glowing ball of plasma, held together by its own gravity.

Sun
The star at the middle of our Solar System, around which Earth and the other planets orbit.

supermassive black hole
A black hole with a mass more than 100,000 times the mass of the Sun.

supernova
An enormous explosion marking the death of a star much more massive than the Sun.

telescope
A device used to observe distant objects by detecting the light or other energy they give off or reflect. An optical telescope uses mirrors and lenses to collect and focus light.

visible light
The portion of electromagnetic radiation that human eyes can see.

volcano
A hole in a planet or moon's surface through which lava can spill out.

water
A substance made of oxygen and hydrogen atoms. Water is essential for life as we know it.

wavelength
The distance between the peaks of waves of energy.

white dwarf
The dense, burnt-out core of a star like the Sun, collapsed to the size of Earth, but still intensely hot.

Index